MW00324136

Kudos for Paul Alexander

"A humorous commentary on life about a child from newborn (pre-emie in Alexander's case) through age five. People at any stage of parenthood will be able to relate and enjoy the entertaining thoughts and actions from Paul Alexander. A page-turner from a comedian that will have you comparing your own experiences and relating to the good and not-so-good times of parenthood."

– Rachel Dehning, *Seattle Book Review*

"Paul has a poet's gift for packing big truths into short punches. If this book can entertain and move a childless grump like me, you know it's something special."

- Rian Johnson, Writer, Director of *Looper*,
Star Wars: The Last Jedi, *Knives Out*

"From pithy tweet-sized observations to hilarious heart-wrenching essays, Paul Alexander brings a fresh, honest, and edgy look to the world of parenthood. If David Sedaris and Tina Fey had a love child, this book would be it. Brutal, blunt and bombastic, Alexander uses his sharp wit to bring out the best things about being a brand new dad, even when he's failing miserably at it."

- Brent Piaskoski, TV Producer and Creator

"They say don't meet your heroes. I've decided to make Paul's son my hero so I won't feel obliged to meet him. That kid is trouble! The way I see it, reading this book is way more enjoyable than having a kid. So, the choice is yours."

– Mike Gandolfi, Actor, Emmy-winning comedy writer

". . . full of laughs and giggles and any parent will take a trip back in time to the horrifying actions of their own children—second-hand chewing gum, food landing on the floor, fights in the play park, attacks on household pets; yes, it all comes back with alarming clarity."

- Lucinda E. Clarke, *Readers' Favorites*

"Alexander's book is a beautifully crafted reminder that the great over-arching narrative of parenthood is actually a collection of individual moments. Our Baby Was Born Premature is filled with the everyday moments of joy, frustration, wonder, self-doubt, triumph and pure, unconditional love that every parent experiences recounted with wit, charm, and affection."

- Rob Nickerson, Managing Director, robnickersonimprov.com

"Alexander's 'memoir' is absolutely unique. It is skillfully delivered in short, humorous vignettes with punch lines you can never predict and an authenticity that anyone who has ever birthed and raised a child of either sex—premature or full-term—ill immediately appreciate. If you need a gift for parents—or grandparents—of any age, send them the hardcover edition of this gem."

- Don Sloan, *Publishers Daily Reviews*

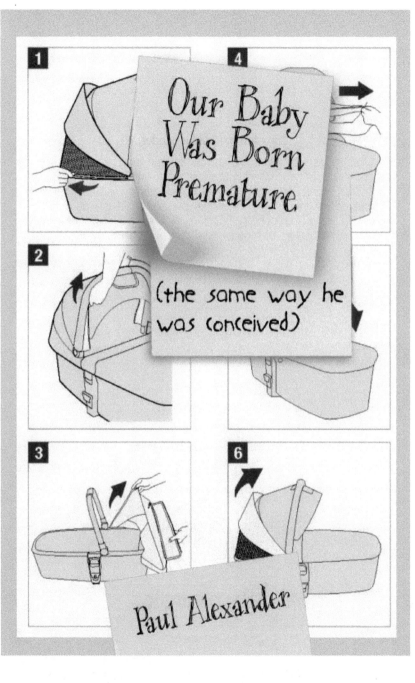

ISBN: 978-1-7327097-6-8
Run Amok Books, 2019
First Edition

RunAmok

Printed in the USA

For Sean and Scarlett

YEAR 1

"All babies crawl. Especially when you are not looking."

- Peter H. Dolan, M.D.

PREGNANT

During the ultra sound we looked at the monitor as the nurse whipped the stick around my wife's belly, which had jelly all over it. There it was—like a tiny alien ghost on the screen. She cried. Not the nurse. My wife. I stared. The nurse stopped the picture momentarily and announced, "It's a boy."
There was a freeze frame of the alien ghost in profile with a huge appendage that went halfway across the screen.
I thought, "He's a God."
As it turns out—I was looking at his thigh.

No matter what name I come up with for the baby my wife says, "That's a dog's name."
I started leafing through flower books.
Heliconia. Liliumlongiflorum. Thorn.

There will be no freshly painted baby room out of a Martha Stewart magazine. We have a one bedroom apartment in Hollywood. I wonder how Martha would rearrange the BBQ and lawn chair on my fire escape?

Upon approaching full term my Irish, blonde, pretty, soft-skinned wife, Maggie declared, "I don't just have gas; I have grandfather-in-the-shower gas."

PREMATURE BIRTH

Maggie called me at work and told me she was going into labor. I told her the first thing that came into my non-medical mind at that moment.
"No you're not."

During birth a mother's cervix dilates to ten centimeters in width (that's four inches for all the carpenters). This finally puts to rest the male belief that size matters.

A dad's job in the delivery room is to count all the way to ten. My seven years of high school finally paid off.

During contractions Maggie was breathing in rhythm until the RN told her to "push like you're taking a poo."
This information messed up my counting to ten.

A Preemie Doctor (not her professional title) prepped us on what might go wrong with a baby entering the world four weeks early. The thing that stuck out the most was the word, "breathing." At which point I stopped breathing.

The doctor performed an Episiotomy (a surgical cut in the perineum, the muscular area between the vagina and the anus done with no local anesthetic) and while he's snipping, my wife very calmly asks him, "What are you doing?"
To me, this means: BIRTH IS MORE PAINFUL THAN A STRANGER CUTTING YOUR GENITALS WITH A PAIR OF SCISSORS.

If men had to give birth would anybody be here? For guys it would be like urinating a grape fruit. Okay, let's say, golf ball.

I know how to solve teen pregnancy. Stop teaching kids about birth control. Stop teaching kids about body parts. Stop teaching kids about the perils of sexting. All you have to do is arrange an elementary school field trip to a live birth. One caesarean section; teen pregnancy solved. The screaming has nothing to do with love. I witnessed a sublime fluid-covered, four-and-a-half-pound boy come out of the love of my life and at that moment I thought—"I've got to get a job."

Our baby was born premature. The same way he was conceived.

HOSPITAL STAY

Darwin is wrong. It's not fish to monkey to man; fish to bird to monkey to man, maybe.

Our baby was born at Cedars Sinai in Beverly Hills. No matter how far he travels and no matter where he ends up he can always say he started in Beverly Hills and screwed his way down.

First night in the hospital a lot of blood is in my wife's urine. I'm not a fan of blood. I'm not that into urine either. The nurse said it was perfectly normal. If I were an EMT, a lot of people wouldn't make it and the rest would sue.

A rumor in the NICU (Neonatal Intensive Care Unit) was that Pre-emie births were up this year due to more societal stress. Maybe they should lower health insurance. See if that doesn't clean out the Preemie wards?

I ventured into the NICU to view my son and found out you are not allowed into the room unless you wash your hands. All the babies are attached to monitors that regulate their heart rate and oxygen saturation level. The numbers on the screen fluctuate, sometimes wildly. Usually the heart rate bounced around 145 to 160. The oxygen level would stay at 180 and then go to 150 and then back to 180 or maybe that is the heart rate because if the oxygen was over 100 percent, say, 180—wouldn't you blow up?

Our Baby Was Born Premature

A hallway leads you out of the Preemie Ward. Family photos adorn the walls. Usually in groups of two. There's the picture of the day their preemie baby showed up, looking a little bit bigger than a stuffed brown paper lunch bag with an I.V. in their impossibly small ankle, followed by a picture of their kid as a teen playing soccer or graduating high school. It is a crucible to the Cedars staff. There is a lot of love on these walls.

DOCTORS AND NURSES

It's midnight. I'm visiting the baby. A group of nurses had to reposition the I.V. from his ankle into his forehead in order to find a better vein.
"You want to put a needle in my kid's head?"
They said it's better there and the baby can't knock it out, but the nurse couldn't get it in. They called for someone else. Thank goodness for the patient graveyard shift Nightingale who finally got the needle in.
I kept fiddling with a pacifier trying to calm the baby which is like offering a skier who's lying on ice with a bone sticking through his leg, waiting for a Search and Rescue helicopter that can't land because of a snow storm—a Tums.

BREASTS

The first time I saw my wife wearing a breast pump I didn't know whether to get turned on or run out of the room.

It's a contest between the Preemie Dads to see who brings the most mother's milk to the ward. One of the dads told me, "This is my wife's fourth bottle today." That's when I whipped out Maggie's six-pack.

A man looks at breasts differently after he sees his wife breast feed. One day he says to himself, "They are no longer mine."

Mommy decided to take an infant CPR class offered by the hospital and she obliged because the doctor asked her to take it and, hey— they've still got our kid.

When he roots sometimes he shakes his head like a Jack-Russell terrier with a leather shoe. I can't imagine breast feeding. Maggie said, "Thank God he can't walk. He'd take my breasts with him, and after that no shirt would be long enough to cover my tits."

(the same way he was conceived)

CIRCUMCISION

We were invited to a Bris: A sacred, religious rite whereby a parent's newborn son is circumcised in their home. This will be our first Bris. What do you bring—Rugala?

We told the couple hosting the circumcision party that we like to show up to *all* the celebrations because there's always good food. Chances are one of the major religious groups are going to make some mean peanut butter balls.

There's an older couple who live next door and the woman keeps mentioning circumcision to me in passing conversation—like, "I heard the boy down stairs, Daniel, had a good circumcision. They had a very good Mohel." I told Maggie, "If she brings it up to me one more time I'm going to pull mine out and ask, "Should I get a little more off the top?"

You wonder why so many men are full of fear, resentment and mean spirit. The first thing we do to them after they're born is take a knife to their penis. That's got to piss you off for years. It's my excuse.

1 MONTH

It is against the law for a hospital to release a baby to parents who do not have a car seat. The days of taking your kid home in a Safeway shopping cart are over.

One of Sean's grandmas showed up. She's a pro burper, and I mean with the baby.

When I bought my first guitar I realized that everyone had a guitar. This is not necessarily a good thing. The same thing happened when we had a baby.

I used to have three foot stereo speakers and a large record collection. Now I have a small plastic speaker with an antenna on it in the dining room and all I can pick up are squeaky whale sounds from my bedroom.

The first time I changed the baby I arched over him about three inches away from my work. Grandma said she was impressed with my bravery. I stand up straight when I'm changing him now.

Game. "Making the Bed with the Baby in It." To play—you put a baby in the middle of the bed and then you throw a sheet over the baby. You say, "Where's the baby?" and then whip the sheet off the baby and say, "There he is!"

(the same way he was conceived)

Send out birth announcements and you'll get loot. A woman in her 90s from England sent us a wool cap she had knit and a woman in her 80s in Canada originally from England sent us a wool blanket. What's up with old English ladies and wool?

People like sending you colorful balls, too.

I saw a man in the alley below our bedroom window urinating on the wall next to the dumpster. The good news: my kid will learn how to pee standing up.

He has several mouths. One of the mouths makes a nearly perfect O. Another one is the turtle mouth. He just clamps shut in a pout when he has had enough food, "Nope." Turtle. This always amazes me because his brain is about as developed as a turtle. I mean, a turtle on its back can use as much brain power as it wants—it's still not going anywhere. And yet the baby defies me.

Baby formula smells ghastly. The price is the same.

My wife asked me, "Do you think I'm fat?"
I flinched, "No!" She snarled, "Good answer."

Daddy couldn't find any new-born pants so Sean is wearing one year old pants that come up to his chest. My baby looks like a golfer on the Seniors Circuit.

If you're setting the baby down on the washing machine during the rinse cycle to try and get him to burp then it's time to give the baby to mommy.

Babies make you advocate more. We've given our landlord about $70,000 in the last five years for rent. I asked them about the simple interest on our security deposit, which is owed to all tenants living in rent controlled buildings in Los Angeles county. We've never seen any interest on our deposit in five years. It comes to $400.00 and change.

They sent us an Eviction Notice. According to their letter we have less than 30 days to vacate. We told our lawyer about our land-lords and the eviction notice we received. It is better that a law firm sends the letter because they use words like, "corroborate," "ordinance," "reasonable demand," and "must pay."

The letter I wanted to write started, "Dear Pigs."

Mommy's game. "How many kisses to tell you how much I love you? Is it one kiss? (gives him a kiss) No, that's not enough. How many kisses to tell you how much I love you? Is it two kisses? (gives him two kisses) No, that's not enough. How many kisses to tell you how much I love you? Is it three kisses? (gives him three kisses) No, that's not enough."

I think I saw Maggie get to nine one night.

(the same way he was conceived)   II

2 MONTHS

Maggie called me at work and told Sean to say, "Hi." He belched into the phone.

Mom tried a new burping method today; now she needs to get a water-proof watch.

The other day while on my shoulder he vomited so much our cat went over to investigate the carpet. The cat decided it was already chewed and moved on.

"Every time the baby spits milk on me I'm going to get a glass of milk and spit on him."
I better shut the door when that voice comes a calling.

I come home from my day job to work all night at my baby job and my wife leaves her all day baby job to work at her night job. The baby is going to learn that in order for parents to love their kid they have to stay away from their kid.
In the morning Maggie asked how it went. I told her, "It was like opening the bedroom door and seeing the baby standing in his crib bug-eyed, using the world's smallest hula-hoop while spitting milk in streams—for six hours. And then saying to him, 'Thank you.'"

You know you have lost the latest argument with your wife when you say, "Oh yeah. Well, you gave birth all wrong."

"The baby sleeps in the bottom drawer or upside down in the closet with his hands calmly crossed on his chest."

"It's faster when we wash the baby with a garden hose on the front lawn."

Giving our friends who don't have babies wrong information tends to break up the day.

I've got to stop calling my baby son "Bunny." What happens in first grade during roll call?

"Sean?"

No arm raised.

"Sean?"

Still, no arm raised.

"Sean?"

Nothing. Bunny just sits there.

On the third day since I quit my job without telling anyone, there was a knock on my door. I looked through the peep-hole and saw Common Sense standing in the hall. I let him in. He told me to arrange a "leave of absence" and under California law an employer has to give you up to three months for infant care. They don't have to pay you though. Common Sense then told me my HMO was $180 a month NOT INCLUDING the company's portion—$2/3$. I thanked Common Sense for dropping by. On his way out I asked him if there was anything he could do about landlords who charge $1,500 a month for a one bedroom apartment in a neighborhood where police choppers hover above your street? He said he'd get back to me.

We bought earplugs and a bottle of vodka for our downstairs neighbor.

(the same way he was conceived)   13

Is it sensible to have a mobile above a baby crib constantly playing "Winnie the ... Pooh?"

When I argue with my wife, she waits a few days and then gets back at me by buying things. It was another rough week with no sleep, and we now have a new sofa and arm chair.

Women talk to each other about their husbands instead of talking to their husbands about their husbands.

Tonight the apartment looks like news reel footage after a tornado has ripped through a trailer park. Clothes, toys, and towels everywhere. The baby is going through a sobbing exorcism in the bedroom. Maggie comes in late from work and I look like one of those crazy white meth guys on *Cops* opening a screen door to greet the police.

Babies are the ultimate protection. They're like armor. Cars, carts, skateboarders, and bikers stop and let me cross. Gang-members part on a sidewalk and let the stroller through. A hobo camp huddled in the alcove of a parking structure call out to me, "What is it?" I say, "A boy."
They grin pinching their cigarettes, "Congratulations!"

The hospital sent us a bill for our baby's hospital stay. $248,000.00 There are some bills you receive where the only response is laughter.

You can tell a new dad by how he reacts to losing the baby pacifier. He frantically checks himself like a crucifix; forehead, belly, over the heart left, over the heart right!

Is it wrong when you can't sleep at 3 A.M and you're watching shopping channels wondering if you should masturbate to *Body By Jake*?
The problem is they keep cutting away from the ladies working out to Jake, and that guy never shuts up.

(the same way he was conceived)

3 MONTHS

Babies make parents compete with each other. "Hey, is it normal for a baby's ears to be twice the size of his head—because they are on the neighbor's kid? That baby has his daddy's nose, his mother's eyes, and a rabbit's ears."

The plumber was here to fix the sink. He saw me feeding Sean. It wasn't long before he told me about his baby and then showed me a tattoo on his arm of his baby girl's hand. How do I compete with that?

Reebok shoes marketing to new parents with Weebok shoes. That's pretty good.

Women have superpowers. Giving birth. Producing food for a baby. And what is my super power? I can pee on bushes.

I keep putting on his onesies backwards so the feet flaps are facing behind him. I can't seem to get used to the tiny snap-button clothes either. It's like I'm eating sushi while wearing boxing gloves.

A newborn's cry sounds like a Skill-saw cutting through a sheet of plywood.

While Mommy's breast feeding, the baby usually falls asleep at the bar. The way it works is.

"Waah!" Lift him up out of his crib and put him on your shoulder.

"Waah!" Sit him in the rocking chair.

"Waah!" Put him on a blanket on the floor.

"Waah!" Put him on the boob. "Wa -- hmm."

Our Baby Was Born Premature

There are days when you don't eat. The best present you can give new parents is prepared food. Stop with the primary colored toys. Food.

When you take care of a newborn, you don't even have time to microwave.

A newborn sits around most of the time in a wet wedgy, and we wonder why they cry.

Today the baby is a trumpet with legs.
Putting him in the Baby Bjorn (a cool backpack for babies) and taking him outside usually works like the Spock nerve from the early Star Trek series.

Sean hasn't had a number 2 in forty eight hours. I never thought I'd miss the baby's poo.

The microwave doesn't heat anything. The cat puked all over the kitchen floor and the baby hasn't shit in three days. I found a dead mouse in the bedroom under some socks and it looked like it was dead for about a week.

Constipation day four. The antidote is Prune juice. It's such a good antidote I had to wake Mommy up while I was changing Sean's diaper in the middle of the night and say, "Hey, you've got to see this."

(the same way he was conceived)

Grandpa is visiting from Canada and he's constipated. He ate a Metamucil cookie and drank some water. An hour later he had success. The baby is on low iron formula. He had success, too. People end up just like they start out. Grunting.

Sean held on to his bottle for the first time with his tiny right hand. As far as his father was concerned, you would think he just passed the Bar exam.

My wife snarled, "What kind of man quits his job when he has a newborn baby?"
I told her I was going back to work on Tuesday, and then she burst into tears: "You're trying to sabotage my career! You can't go back to work!"
We started yelling at one another. I sort of noticed she was holding out the phone while I spewed incoherent, abominable phrases. And I found out later it was recorded on my parent's voice mail. A low blow and yet, ingenious. The after-fight time is sort of like when birds come out at the end of a vicious rain storm. There's a reason they say that after you're cremated the heart is the last thing to go.

We got out of the quarter-million-dollar baby bill. Maggie photo-copied my pay check and sent a nice letter to Cedars Sinai. I guess they figured, "How are we going to collect from a guy who picks turnips at the stupid farm?"

Our Baby Was Born Premature

4 MONTHS

Nobody can remember breast feeding because if we could—well, I don't even want to think about it.

The doctor says Baby needs his sleep now to develop his mind. It's been a week since he told me this, and so far the only new developments are streaming tears and a squeaking sound. Perhaps the doctor needs more sleep.

Sean threw up all day. He would cry and then stare at you peacefully—but it was just so he could catch his breath and throw up on you again.

It's useless trying to protect your furniture. Baby will find a spot to spit on. The latest effort is what I call, "my station." On the new armchair I have carefully laid out half a dozen diapers, two pacifiers, two towels (for over the shoulder burping,) an extra towel close by —and two bibs. I'm ready. It's not enough. I've always got a towel over my shoulder. People have asked me if I own a parrot.

I discovered it is possible for a newborn to take a dump and actually vibrate on your lap.

Turns out they put the same stuff in diapers that they put in Kotex so the next time Mommy burps the baby I was thinking of putting a Kotex on her shoulder. But that's the kind of idea that has to come from her.

(the same way he was conceived) 19

They have these "swing chairs" with mobiles over them designed to keep the baby peacefully occupied. They don't work. The swing chair should really be called the "vomit chair." I found out the real purpose of these chairs is to give Dad time to put his pants on.

This baby has more outfits than the Queen of England.

This morning he is a worm in a Onesie. You want to hog tie them but you can't so you just end up stealing a few moves from the WWE and push forward.

He acts like a drunk leaving a bar at 2 a.m. Bottles lying on the floor. He hurls. He's yelling at everyone. I'm closing all the windows so we don't bother the neighbors.

Daddy had his favorite T-shirt on: A guy lying on the ground wearing a party hat and the caption "Party Till You're Homeless." And just when I thought the shirt was going to survive the day, Sean killed it and then fell asleep.

Since meeting Sean my father calls a lot more and gives me advice about the baby. Simple 1950s homegrown remedies like, "You don't need a car seat—he'll be alright—Christ, I was in the War. I drove an ammunition truck through a mine field at 70 miles an hour."
My mother, on the other line somewhere else in their house: "You didn't drive an ammunition truck, you hid under an ammunition truck during a mortar attack, which is the worst place you could be during a mortar attack."
"Be quiet Rhoda, its damn near the same thing."

I always throw my parents some curve balls, "After five months I realized you're supposed to use a nipple—not give him milk right from the carton."

And, "At the doctor's office Sean got two more immunization shots and he acted like such a baby."

There's no use trying to visit other new parents once you have become a parent. Why pretend? The typical scenario is that you make plans to visit each other, and then cancel your plans later in the day.

New Mothers who are friends love the baby debating game. These Mothers are usually quoting a book. One of Maggie's friends has a baby girl. She also has a degree in clinical psychology and works as a corporate planner. She is qualified to be the baby debating team captain. She admitted to color-coordinating the pacifiers with her baby's outfits. I could never imagine anything like that. Her child will probably rebel and move to another continent but still call mom at home every day.

Never mistake passion for a woman getting a Charlie horse in her leg.
Woman: "Ohh my Gawd. No!"
Man: "Yes, yes?"
She rolls off crying, "Owwww!"

Today I caught a glimpse of myself in the mirror. I was holding a purple stuffed kangaroo which has a sound box in it of a "boingy" hopping song. I don't like sound boxes in toys. Mozart shouldn't come out of a stained blue rhinoceros that's dangling over a chair.

(the same way he was conceived)

Today we took the baby to Chinatown because there are so many things hanging from the ceilings there.

You know what would be handy? Really small tear-away stripper clothes.

Three women bent over the stroller this afternoon as Sean stared up at them. It's like he was thinking, "Hey, Smorgasbord, smorgasbord!"

The baby takes all my concentration. I haven't shaved in a week and my toenails are so long I had to slow down when I walked today.

It's one o'clock in the afternoon and I am still in my underwear frantically eating a bowl of cereal.

The baby has increased sleeping at night to six hours. This means I have fewer thoughts of driving my car over the leaf blower guy who starts his job at 7 a.m.

You cannot watch TV and bottle feed at the same time. I looked back down and it was like he had a cream pie in his face.

Time with a newborn is like running the marathon and collapsing across the finish line and then being told you're at the start.

Maggie's hair was wet and she put it in a pony tail because she couldn't be bothered to look for a comb. She was wearing one of my short sleeved t-shirts and said, "I know new mom's are not supposed to wear horizontal stripes but I'm too tired to do laundry." She'll be wearing track pants to the mall soon.

I snapped a picture of Sean sleeping on our bed. He looked intoxicated and sprawled across the comforter. I called the picture, "bed hog."
I guess men start that stuff early.

Transferring a sleeping baby from stroller to crib is done with the same cautious intensity as diffusing a bomb.
"Don't cut the blue wire!"

Found a clear gelatinous pustule on his scrotum. Maggie used warm water on a washcloth and cleaned the infected area. That seemed to get it off and resulted in a slight redness. We thought about airing it out a little too.
Later we took Sean out for a stroll. Mommy wondered why he was out cold. I had to tell her, "He just had a boil removed from his balls and you wonder why he's passed out. I think I'm going to pass out.

When you have a boy you worry about one dick. When you have a girl you must worry about every dick.

I visited this couple and they had a nine-year-old boy. All boys seem to have one thing in common. Dirt. It might be better to keep kids outside; as long as you install a kid door.

(the same way he was conceived)

This evening I lifted Sean out of the baby seat and he was no longer a baby. He was a boulder.

One of Maggie's friends took her baby to a talent agent. The agent told her the baby was too tall and thin to be a size model. Translation: The kid's got a weird shaped head.

5 MONTHS

Maggie said, "The pregnant pooch is like a drunk at a party. The first to show up and the last to leave."

I don't get the mall-photography family portraits on people's mantles, where everyone's smiling like a suppository will fall out of their butt at any moment. A woman we know sent a picture of her baby, at the mall, sitting in a flower. Why do so many parents take such bad photos of their children and then send them to you?
This means I have another picture on the fridge sent by parents I don't ever want to hang out with. Of course, if someone wanted to put our baby in a print ad—I'd sell him out in a second.

"I am never going to Disneyland or Chuck E. Cheese's! "
Maggie and her friends just smile wryly and say, "Sure, Paul."

My wife got laid off. I went back to my Lunch Pail Joe job. This would be considered a "day job" which in any other town is an honorable way to make a living. In Hollywood, where everyone has written a movie script, it is considered monkey-stink failure. Three hours on the job and one of the guys I work with took a phone call. He didn't look too happy. I asked him, "What's going on?"
He said, "My brother and his fiancée had a fight. She's pregnant, and he slit his wrists. He's in the hospital."
Maggie really has a sick sense of humor, which is one of the reasons I married her. I walked in the door that night and told her what happened, and she said, "You never slit your wrists for me."

(the same way he was conceived)   25

Maggie took the baby to the pediatrician this morning and he got not one, not two, but three shots. She called me at work at the beginning of the day while she was leaving the hospital—a desperate plea in her voice, "You have to come home. Sean cried so much he arched his back!"

I calmed her down and told her I couldn't come home.

Maggie called at 11 a.m. and told me to come home. Among other things she said—"I can't take it anymore."

Sean was screaming in the background. I calmed her down and told her I couldn't come home yet.

Maggie called at 3 p.m. and told me, "Sean won't let me touch him!" He was making a loud, prolonged, high pitched protest in the background.

I consoled her and told her I would try to get out of work.

Maggie called me at 5 p.m. and told me to bring home beer.

I related Sean's visit to get the immunization shots to a guy at work. He jeered and said that his baby daughter never cries when she gets her shots.

I told him, "I guess she's on her way to becoming a heroin addict."

I wanted him to stand but then I realized it might not be a great idea because his feet are a few inches long and his head is the size of a soccer ball.

I got home from work at 3 a.m. You know you've worked too much when you get into bed without taking your clothes off.

I awoke to a camera flashing and Sean gurgling next to my head while squeezing a squeaky plastic dog as more flashes exploded. Maggie was snickering, "I want him to think he's a star."

Time to visit my in-laws. I tried to get the baby seat, the stroller, and the luggage into the trunk of my 15 year old Mazda 323 that hasn't been washed in three weeks. Feeling self-conscious, I tried to apply simple geometry to getting the luggage, the baby seat, and the stroller into the trunk. Maggie grabbed the stroller and tried to show me how to do it faster, but I turned into a mule—and a stroller tug of war ensued.

The trunk finally closed and as we got into the car Maggie told the wide-eyed baby in the back seat, "It's okay, Sean. You're going to meet the smart side of the family."

At the airport, the baby seat that goes into the stroller was FAA approved for baggage claim. The Graco stroller with the air filled rubber wheels is the way to go. Mothers like it for its safety features. Fathers like it because of its smart wheels.

It was time for my wife to board. I kissed her goodbye and told my son, "Poo your pants during lift off."

Wife's away. What to do? Drink the milk from my cereal bowl. Eat all the things she has banned, like pork tenderloin. Try not to die from alcohol poisoning so our starving cat won't begin eating me.

A few days later at the airport—I see him. Ah, my beautiful baby boy. He's back! And—he's totally ignoring me.

The first time I fed the baby cereal I was holding the smallest spoon in the world and said the correct thing, which of course is, "Bunny say, awe."

I pushed it at the baby but he hadn't swallowed yet from the first spoonful.

Force feeding a baby is as effective as shaking a can of coke and opening it. He's going to have a binge eating disorder.

(the same way he was conceived) 27

When family and friends try to tell me who the baby takes after, I always tell them, "He got all the smart parts from his mom and the bottom lip from me."

Quite often when you hold him he whips his head over the right shoulder, and then whips back to the left—like he's tracking a rodent along the baseboard.

We took Sean out for his "before going to bed" walk. Sometimes a nice Los Angeles walk can cheer you up: the palm trees, the squirrels chattering, the homeless man from the alley giggling and calling the baby a warlock.

A couple we know from down the street passed us on their way to El Carmen, a neighborhood bar. They said it had been a bad week and they were off to have a couple of margaritas. Pushing the stroller we told them, "Be careful, that's how this whole thing got started."

The baby furniture store called us and told us our custom-made "Crib for Life" was in. It came in a box. It reminded me of Ikea. Every time you get their stuff home the one screw you need to fit everything together is missing. And it's irreplaceable. It only fits into a strange auger bit hole made by a drill that doesn't exist anymore. People buy furniture at Ikea because they're new parents on a budget or because they're naive college students who think it looks cool. One day there will be an Ikea car with nice cubby-holes in the doors but you can't go more than 20 miles per hour without destroying the balsa wood frame.
But we didn't go to Ikea. We went to an expensive designer baby furniture store in West Hollywood, and the furniture still came in a box. Anything in a box means there will be instructions. These instructions are as easy to understand as a Chinese income tax return.

I let Mommy's amazing powers of figuring shit out take over. An hour later, there was our beautiful cherry wood finished "Crib for Life."

I asked her how she did it? It turns out the secret is to do some other task while assembling it—like talking on the phone.

Let's hope Sean doesn't decide to make the "Crib for Life" a "Crib for the Week." There are already teeth marks on the head board. Mr. Kinky?

What does it mean when you leave home for work in the morning and its dark outside, and then you leave work to drive home at night and its dark outside. If you're working for someone else long enough for the Earth to rotate entirely, you need to find a new job.

I can't remember what started this (I think it had something to do with the placement of the alarm clock?) but as I lay in bed in the morning Maggie said, "Maybe you'd listen to me if I stuck a knife in your throat."

(the same way he was conceived)

6 MONTHS

Always feed the baby *after* playing airplane.

Never mix up horse radish for baby's rice cereal.

There is a Kindergarten in our Hollywood hood. $20,000 a year. BMW's drop their kids off. It's got the word *Academy* in it. The kids are five. What are they doing in Kindergarten? Taking naps. Drawing with crayons. Looking at picture books. I never went to a Kindergarten with the word *Academy* in it and look at me. I ended up taking naps, drawing with crayons, and looking at picture books.

Maggie can really go into nerd mode. She can sit at the computer for hours. Days. I opened the bedroom door. The baby was propped up on our bed—at the opposite end of the room. I asked her what a hand mirror was doing on her computer desk and she said she holds it up every now and then and says, "Hi" to the baby.

The symptoms of Meningitis: sudden high fever, severe persistent headache, neck stiffness, discomfort in bright lights, drowsiness and joint pain. The same way I feel at Playland at McDonalds.

Today I saw our angel with rice cereal all over his body pass a green stool in the bath water.

Our Baby Was Born Premature

I drove by an oil refinery and saw a nursery school set up in the work place.

In the midst of acres of piping and storage tanks was a little 20-foot-square park with a slide and plastic tunnels. Mom and dad can take the kid to work and the whole family can throw a beach ball back and forth while enjoying the fresh scent of crude oil.

It's impossible to talk on the phone with a baby in the room. Your conversations are like the fiery L.A. friend you bump into on the street who cuts you off in mid sentence to scream at her dog.
"It was great to—No, Brody! Sit down! Now!"

Baby's new habit. Grabbing his bib, ripping it off, and trying to throw it at the closest human target. I actually heard the Velcro behind his neck tearing once.

My wife told me, "In the morning before you leave for work please be calm with the child. This way he gets his nap time."
Apparently my fathering skills are like the guy who instigates a full on bar-fight and then quickly exits out the back door.

(the same way he was conceived)   31

CANADIAN CONSULATE

In the evening I put on my brand new bathrobe received from a fine mail order clothing company. I shuffled around the apartment and came to the kitchen door. Through the screen I could see below me on the street a young man with his hands on his head getting arrested by three cops drawing guns.

The next day I decided to visit the Canadian Consulate in order to immigrate. I'm a Dual Citizen which is completely different than a Bi Citizen and probably not as good.

The Canadian Consulate is in downtown L.A. A place you must leave before the sun goes down or you will be killed by being eaten. There is only one person at the Canadian Consulate. After waiting all morning in line, I managed to get a number out of the over-worked clerk—for someone in BUFFALO. The person in Buffalo said I should start by getting a passport.

I wandered around 7th and Los Angeles St. and Santee Alley. In the alleys below these beautiful turn of the century buildings that in some cases are condemned is a world teeming with culture. A world that has no idea there is a recession going on. A world where you can buy, as I like to call it, an original "Soko" watch. It's the wholesale world and it's not in any airlines brochure.

My phone rang and it was Maggie. We continued our discussion from the night before; the one about not jacking up the baby when I come home. I told her I was in Santee Alley and put the phone up to a bunch of yapping wind-up toy Chihuahuas. I ended up at a building on Wilshire Blvd. and 7th St. to get my passport photos taken. I was going on 36 hours with no sleep. While still working things out with Maggie on the phone I asked the man at the photo place for a mirror and used my hand for a comb. The pictures were snapped just after Maggie told me to see a therapist.

If you look at the passport photo, it looks like the guy in the picture had rolled around in a campfire for two days.

7 MONTHS

Is there anything scarier than an obese man in pajamas losing control of four of his own children entering a K-Mart?

If Maggie goes back to work we are going to need a babysitter. I saw a piece of paper tacked up at the Laundromat with pen scrawl on it: "Haviar. Babysit. Have car."
Yes. There is something scarier than an obese man in pajamas losing control of four of his own children entering a K-Mart.

Maggie saw to it that I took Sean to the doctor's office for his new round of shots. She wanted the baby to hate me for the day instead of her.

Baby had a fever. We gave him Kid's Tylenol and I said it smelled like bubble gum. Mommy told me you are NEVER supposed to let kids know this kind of information. I'm like that do-gooder grand-mother that thinks buying iced cookies with a best before date of two years from now for her grand kid—is a sign of love.

We have too many chewable nursery rhyme books. They are made of cloth so you can wash them. Half of the books have cat hair in them. The trick is to throw old baby books out a little bit at a time without your wife noticing.

In a baby-against-a-coffee-table contest—the coffee table always wins.

We keep seeing babies Sean's age who are GIANTS. Women giving birth to 11-pound baby-men. My toes curled just thinking about that coming at you in the middle of the night to breast feed.

(the same way he was conceived)   33

Sean's not crawling but he is rolling everywhere. We make sure to keep the door to the alcove staircase closed.

He is holding his bottle with both hands. Occasionally you'll hear a clunk and then you have to help him point the bottle back into the right hole.

If you lay out a blanket on the floor for a baby, they always decide to play somewhere else.

Sean rolled over today from back to front and then went on his back again, and he looked up at us, panting and sweating. He was so happy he finally did it after working on it for a month—he passed out.

Maggie's friend has a daughter who's a little older than Sean and it looks like she's going to skip the whole crawling stage and go straight to walking. Apparently, when they put her on her stomach for tummy time she screams until they lift her up. Maggie said, "Well—that makes sense since girls don't like to get dirty."

You crawl then you learn to walk. And one day you get a job and you learn to crawl again.

A HOUSE IN CANADA

I called Maggie and told her I was considering buying a house in Canada that I found on the Internet. She said she was standing in the kitchen and heard a sucking sound behind her and that Sean was chewing on both his fists like they were little ice cream cones. Guess that means I can book a flight.

A lot of Americans don't know anything about Canada. My L.A. neighbor looked over his fence and said, "I'm so sick of this country. I'm packing up my stuff and moving south—to Canada."

At Customs, the border guards love it when you say, "Officer whatever you do please don't take my jar of insects."

The house is in a town in the middle of Vancouver island. I could move to this town because it has little things that L.A. doesn't have, like air and water. I met a couple who live here and they told me they were going to move to a smaller island. Like Vancouver island isn't remote enough. Turns out there are little hippie islands everywhere up here—600 people on the whole island. Everyone gets their water from a fjord. They're playing hacky sack with the mayor. Their house is built out of kale. I admire people who can survive on tiny islands. I didn't know what a sump pump was until I drove up here. I came into town seeing signs on front lawns like *Sand blaster for sale*, *Used Bobcat*. The local job listings had things like, *Chicken gutters needed*. I'm thinking, "All I have is improv comedy experience."
I'm like the guy in the middle of a circle of wolves and I'm waving the burning ember of a stick that's about to go out to keep the wolves away and also heat my cappuccino in my hand at the same time. In a power outage, I run out of my house and open my car door for light so I can finish my book. How will I survive?

Upon opening their local paper I saw an ad for the town butcher named Pete. It said, "Nobody Beats Pete's Meat!" And there was another ad in the paper that said, "Ladies Night at Home Hardware." Are ladies going down there and having fun with a paint stripper? And is Pete the entertainment?

The old Craftsman House I want to buy sits in a quiet neighborhood according to the realtor. My neighbor to the left has an F150. My neighbor to the right has an F250 and the neighbor across the street has the biggest pickup truck; it just says, F U.

I looked at my neighbor's yard on the other side of the dirt alley behind me and wondered how Martha Stewart would rearrange his refrigerator?

The graffiti is friendlier in Canada. On the side of a train someone had painted *Kill the Man*. And under that they had written *this paint is water soluble*.

I was in town for the Fall Fair. Not a big fan. Too much livestock walking around. And then there's the animals. I went into the Haunted House. That ride is called, Porta Potty. And the people operating the rides look like the bad end of a pin-head fight. What happens if he leaves the lever to go pound someone while I'm up there turning?
I saw a grandmother that looked like she had been blood let pushing a fully occupied FOUR SEAT BABY STROLLER. Instead of a seat belt, it should come with a chastity belt. There's a new exhibit —someone built a miniature Noah's Ark which sat on a trailer complete with toy animals. The kids could walk around in it. A guy was handing out pamphlets about God. I asked him, "Who built it, and don't say 'Noah?'"

Our Baby Was Born Premature

Canada's election draws near. There are four people running for Prime Minister and the rest of the country is running away. Their House of Commons has nothing in common.

I told a local I was thinking of buying in town. He told me the town was rated second for the most alcohol related hospital visits. I assured him, "That's a ridiculous statistic; next year we're making a comeback; we'll be number 1."

Some of the people in this town are racist about geography.
A guy asked me, "Where's your house?"
Me: "On Third Ave."
Guy: "Oh, that's a bad area of town. I would never live there."
Me: "Oh, yeah—where do you live?"
Guy: "We live on 4th Ave."

There's East Coast Time, Mountain Central Time, West Coast Time, and small town Canada time—which is about 1951.

Everything is big up here. The trees, the rain drops, the mountains, the mortgages.

The town is the gateway to the Pacific Rim national forests and is surrounded by snow capped mountains. I sat on the curb in front of the house at 11 p.m. The night sky at this parallel is like a kaleidoscope. I felt like the last man on Earth until a lean white cat came over to say hello. He did this by rubbing his head against my closed fist, purring.

(the same way he was conceived)

On the way back to the mainland aboard the BC Ferry I stood outside on the deck at the very front of the ferry with the thundering wind in my face and decided I would not tell any Americans about the jewel I had found.

"Oh, you don't want to go to Canada. It's nothing but bumper to bumper Zambonies."

8 MONTHS

Maggie said, "He learns what love is by watching his parents."
The way I see it—if Mom and Dad yell at one another, he will abuse his future relationships. If Mom and Dad show their affection for each other, he will probably abuse his future relationships but at least we'll be off the hook.

Our landlord was outside standing on an extension ladder, fixing a second story window. He was using both hands to fasten the window. At that moment Maggie suggested exploding a balloon behind his ear.

A great way to get your wife to pay attention to you is to pick up one of your baby photo albums and leaf through them. Back in the day when I wanted to pick up girls, I would take a box of kittens into the middle of a dance floor.

Sean loves to lie on his tummy in the *ready, set* position. He just doesn't *go*. He's like the snake inside a can of nuts.

I went to my first, first-birthday party. All I remember is a plastic pool filled with primary colored plastic balls and thinking about urine.

At the market today, I remembered the time when I was a neophyte parent. Maggie was pregnant and it was critical to get water "in glass bottles only! It's safer for the baby."
They are very hard to find (I drove all over town,) and expensive. I did it for a month—and one night Maggie handed me one of the bottles from the Swiss Alps or somewhere and said, "It tastes stale." We stopped with that nonsense. And there are toys, like at the doctor's office, that we would never have let Sean touch six months ago for fear of germs. But now he can knock himself out.

(the same way he was conceived) **39**

The baby crawled to where the cat was sitting. And then the cat went, "Psych," and got up and walked away.

Our neighbor, Bob, told me he had a lot of fun dragging his one year old, Jacob, by his legs toward him. Then he discovered afterwards that Jacob's entire back had rug burn. Daddy Day Care warning shot.

The good news is Sean said, "Dadda." The bad news is—he won't stop saying it.

I went to the Hollywood farmers market this morning with the baby at Hollywood and Vine. I go to see if I can tell the difference between the people and the fruits and nuts.
Honey, fish, free-range poultry and eggs, bison meat, gouda cheese, olives, mushrooms, salads, sprouts, jams, jellies, fruit juices, specialty sauces and dips, dried fruit and nuts, breads and espresso. And they have free tastings and helium balloons.
There's also street musicians there. One of the street musicians (this guy who had a guitar, wore a cowboy hat, and looked to be around 70) said, "What a beautiful baby! What's his name?"
I told him, "Sean."
He laughed, looked at Sean and launched into a very loud song, "Oh, nice to meet you—John Robert, John Robert."
Completely deaf but it didn't matter.
I stopped the stroller in front of a bluegrass quartet. I wanted Sean's ears to get used to real musical instruments and hear the miracle of the human voice in harmony.
He cried because he dropped the strawberry he had been working on. Only to a baby is one berry a meal.
On the way across Hollywood Blvd. a tall man in a dress with ghastly rouge makeup covering his long, old face passed us. He was wearing an acrylic blonde wig. He was carrying a violin case and adjusting his bra. And I thought I was having a bad day.

Sean crawled toward me and tried to untie my shoelace. I told Maggie, "He takes after you."

Maggie said, "No—if he tied your shoe laces together he'd take after me."

9 MONTHS

I paid $4 for a bottle of "Smart-water" and after I drank it I decided I would never pay for that again—so I guess it works.

Today we celebrated "Upside Down Baby Day." Sometimes kids just love hanging upside down.

He's teething. This means he woke up three times last night, crying. The third time, I decided to administer 12-year-old whiskey. I tilted the bottle upside down on my finger and dabbed his bottom gums. He looked at us like he was thinking, "Hey! That's worse than peas."
Maggie video-taped the whole process. I am wearing a gray wrinkled T-shirt. My hair hasn't been cut in months and is astonishingly white/grey in patches and our room looked like it had been ransacked by a gang searching for drugs. On top of all this scenery, I am leaning over my baby with a bottle of 12-year-old Maclanahans whiskey.
It is a video-tape nobody will ever see.

Sean's going for any kind of paper. He loves to destroy brochures too. Give him your electric bill and you'll be dark in a month.

Babies make you do things like leaving the passenger car door open all night while parked on the street.

My mother and my mother-in-law are BOTH going to be staying in our one bedroom apartment for a week. I told my mother whenever we have house-guests our cats bring in mice as welcome presents —so if my mother-in-law offered to sleep on the floor she better say yes, and take the couch.

I went into a store in Manhattan Beach called Bassinettes & Blueberries. I saw a bassinette for $1,375. The infant pajamas started at $76. I left. Those are things you buy for your friends' kids not for your own kids.

There's a catalog from a company that specializes in really good-quality wooden toys for kids. I can't remember the name of the catalog but it should be called, "Everything In Here Is A Choking Hazard."

Sometimes my wife dresses Sean up in a bear-ear hat or curly-cue wizard boots. He stares up at us, "Until I get my motor skills I'm at your mercy."

Elastic pants are perfect for babies. Funny, we end up going right back to them.

Sean is in Grandma's arms. I'm sitting on the floor with coffee. Quiet. My mother remembers when I was Sean's age.
"I wonder now if all your crying at night was because we never gave you milk?"
I tell her, "You mean you starved me?"
She says, "We walked the floor with you."
Apparently right past a closed refrigerator.
My mother is giggling uncontrollably now, "No wonder you didn't throw up that much—we never *fed* you!"
Ha ha ha.

He is up every hour tonight. It's like he's in the Guam time zone. At one point, lying in between us in our bed, he looked at the shadows on the ceiling, and gurgled over and over—obviously communicating with Satan.

(the same way he was conceived)   **43**

Teething is like going bald. There's no cure. Baby Orejel, chamomile herbs, frozen towels ... and my hair still doesn't grow.

It's begun. Sean found his penis.

We bought our first house the same way every couple from our generation with a baby buys their first house. My parents gave us the down payment with the agreement that they would take our souls and we would bow to the command of visiting them each summer just north of Toronto—1,300 miles away.

I flew up to Vancouver Island for the house keys and rented a car. The house was empty and I didn't bring a sleeping bag so I stayed at the Bluebird Motel just down the street. Nice motel. There was a sign in the lobby that said, "Soup of the Day: Whiskey."
If the desk clerk's eyes were any closer together he would be a Cyclops.

I ventured to the community pool. Most of the people there look like they need a life guard before they get in the water.

In Hollywood I get invited to record release parties. In small town Canada, I get invited to prison release parties. I guess there's no difference.

As a renter in Los Angeles, I don't have to fix anything. Now a home owner of a house built in 1942 that needs renovating, my neighbors are getting used to Skill Saws, hammering, and a man shrieking "spiiidahhhh," which ends with a crashing ladder. One neighbor told me only the brown, hairy ones bite and another neighbor said she was bit by a Daddy Long Legs that had a white body. My

Our Baby Was Born Premature

house has an unfinished basement and I must have killed a hundred spiders with a Shop-Vac in front of a good work light. What a great tool. Next, I sprayed Raid around the perimeter of the house and a big, honking, brown spider with an Egyptian mural on its back scurried out, looked at me laughing, and said, "This stuff only gets me high. Do it again and you're dead."

I was in town for the annual Salmon Festival. I told a local fisherman, "Keep spilling nuclear waste and they really will have a Salmon run—with legs—on land."
By the look on his face—he probably thinks I'm a Communist.

One of the last sights I saw in our quaint town in the middle of this beautiful island was a guy with a hook for a hand and another guy with a patch over one eye. Not sure if the injuries are related.

Alas, it was time to return to Lost Angeles.

(the same way he was conceived) 45

10 MONTHS

Sean's doing this thing where he opens his mouth wide and squeals in a constant pitch. What to him must be the sound of Nirvana is to me a cat caught in a fan belt.

Sometimes it takes the strength of Thor to open a jar of baby food.

Baby loves to stand. We lay pillows all around him because he loves to fall over too.

You know you're sleep deprived when you are describing someone's condition and you can't remember the condition and then you remember the condition is called *amnesia*.

I was in the Laundromat sorting whites and colors and adding bleach to the whites. I pulled out a pair of Maggie's panties and they were completely covered in brown liquid. Then I remembered she used her panties to clean up one of Sean's spit-up sessions. The one with Gerber's Chocolate Pudding Dinner—her panties were the closest thing to grab.
I didn't bother explaining that to the woman doing her laundry next to me.
She probably thought, "What a great guy. He must really love the very, very old woman he married."

The baby is making snow angels in the blankets. It's 2 a.m.

Our Baby Was Born Premature

I pull the cover over Sean and say, "Where's the bear in the cave?!" Mommy got up while we were playing and said, "Daddy has morning breath. Instead of 'bear in the cave' it should be 'sardine in a shoe in the cave.'" At least the baby stopped crying.

No matter what direction you point a baby they have other plans. It's like putting a compass next to a magnet.

Sean's mom has a game where she rolls back and forth with him singing, "Washing machine, washing machine."
She then grabs his ankles and hangs him upside down and sings, "And I—hang the baby out to dry!"
She then told Sean he had to kiss her for every hour she was in labor. Five kisses.

Somewhere during all this the baby's first Christmas came and went. I videotaped him crawling over to the coffee table which was stacked neatly with wrapped packages. He threw all of them on to the floor.

(the same way he was conceived)

11 MONTHS

He's been selective about his crying and yelling lately. He's learning to manipulate people.

I put various books into his little hands to see if he was interested. He discarded them on to the floor after tasting them.

He was standing on his pants. Every time he moved they fell further down.

I was thinking about healthy baby food while pouring myself a bowl of Lucky Charms. Is it good to start your day with blue milk?

At the farmer's market, a vendor with a tie-dye non-GMO cotton belt was selling Vegan baked goods and I tried one of his muffins. Their sign should read, "No meat, no eggs, no dairy, no taste."

I waffle between Health Food stores and Sports Bars. There's a Health Food store near us and there's nothing edible. Pills. An entire wall of jars. Horsetail, flax seed powder, birch bark twigs. It's a super market for witches.
Time to go to a sports bar for beer and wings.

Young parents argue about five things:
1. Money
2. Cleaning the house
3. Money
4. Not Listening
5. Money

Our Baby Was Born Premature

My friend at work told me that her daughter just celebrated her second birthday, and two-year-old girls have one thing in common when they get together. Shrieking while running.

Maggie asked me if it looks like she's lost any weight? An impossible question for a man to answer. Say, "no"—you're a jerk. Say, "yes"—you're a jerk who lies.

He fell a lot this week. He has two bruises on his noggin and a bug bite of some kind. Sometimes you have to hide your baby inside like those people who draw the curtains with sunglasses on because they're committing worker's compensation fraud.

Saw a guy at 7-Eleven—in the candy aisle, which is aisles one through six. He was holding a teeny purple plastic garbage can that's actually called *garbage candy* and he was reading the back of it as if he was searching for nutritional information.
"Dude—look around—as far as nutrition goes, you are in the waiting room to Hell."
They say nature repeats itself. Like the ice age. Scientists don't know what killed off the dinosaurs. "It was a comet?" "Drought?" "Volcanoes?"
No. You know what killed them? They had tiny brains. They ate each other to death. That's it. What's so hard to figure out? Their brains were the size of acorns. They didn't have critical thinking capabilities; they were obese lizards. They ate each other. To death. Now it's 300 million years later and I'm in a 7-Eleven. It's happening again.

Maggie has gone from a B to a C cup. She says the only good thing about this is that now she fills out some of her sweaters.

12 MONTHS

Sean kept trying to put his finger in the cat's ass today. The cat always got away. This really freaked me out—but then I rationalized that kids like to push buttons.

The baby's changed the ending to the latest book I'm reading; he tore the last page out.

I had to stuff him in a one piece outfit. He looked like that elderly fitness trainer, Jack LaLanne.

Mommy chases the baby down the hall chanting, "I'm gonna get you, Bunny. I'm gonna get you, Bunny."
I told her when he gets older he's going to need therapy.
She said, "Send me the bill, I'm having fun."

This morning I went out to my car parked on the street and found two tickets on my windshield totaling $165. One of the tickets was for a missing registration sticker, which was in my glove box. The second ticket was for parking on the wrong side of the street—for street cleaning. And they say Los Angeles parking tickets come in threes.
When you have a baby you relate to other parents' pain more easily than when you were a free entity who came and went with no responsibilities other than remembering to put on a jean jacket. A couple of large supermarket chains have been on strike since last fall. You can see the employees in the parking lots with their picket signs. They are trying to get better health care coverage for their families. Sometimes you hear the odd car horn showing their support as commuters drive past the strikers.
How come meter maids never go out on strike?
I would definitely honk if I drove past them.
"That's it—keep striking, motherfuckers."

One of the most painful things a man can do is cut off his own pee flow. I'm in mid stream in the bathroom and I hear, "Here he comes!" I had to cut off my pee flow, and—doubled over—make it to the door just in time to latch it shut.

We don't have a kitchen table because we don't have a kitchen big enough to hold one. We had an old kitchen table in the little dining room that we finally took out to the trash dumpster. We watched two or three derelict souls look at the table—and keep going. Maggie and I are concerned about not "eating together" as a family. Right now Sean's only going to learn that you eat over the sink or out of a bag someone hands you through a window.
We want to get him off formula. He's been voraciously drinking the Similac lactose-free formula for awhile, and we are unsure how to proceed. Cow milk might not be the best option. Maggie said, "I heard we could give him Crocodile meat because it's high in Calcium."
She's been watching Jeopardy again.

Sunday the day of rest has become Sunday the day of a five minute rest. A day we usually clean the apartment, take out the garbage, wash the high chair, stroller, and car seat of all the dead Cheerios—and make sure the baby doesn't kill himself. Sean started the day by popping a yellow crayon in his mouth. I tore the onesie as he squirmed trying to get free in the process he kicked me in the balls, twice. Ten minutes later I was changing him again because he created a cow pie. We gave him a bottle in his crib. After he finished it he started banging it against the slats of his crib and yelling like Al Pacino. "Attica. Attica. Attica!" Amen.

(the same way he was conceived)

The day before Sean's one-year-old birthday—fatigued, with a no-coffee headache, I stumble to the kitchen to start my day.

Maggie informs me, "You left the side of the crib down!"

I felt terrible. The side of his crib was down half the night. There was a chance he could have tried to stand and get out and . . . .

Then—I only made enough coffee for me. My only wife said, "You treat me like I'm your roommate."

I went out to restock the formula because I didn't want Maggie to be stuck in the middle of the day without any. In the car, I realized I'd forgotten my glasses, and the road signs were like looking through a butter smeared window.

I returned to find Sean's mom tossing the cat outside. The cat had bit Sean. He had red marks on his wrist. It didn't break the skin and Sean was more surprised than hurt. Maggie then told me, "You left your mouth wash on the bottom shelf in the living room and I came out just in time to take it away from Sean."

At this rate he's not going make it to one.

I gathered the things I wanted to take to work in my arms. Papers, letters to mail, an extra jacket, and somehow, a tooth brush. I started out the door and Maggie held up my car keys.

"The car is not going very far without these."

I made my way to the car in the gray morning smog and threw my stuff inside. Then I realized I'd forgotten my phone. Back up the stairs and into the apartment. The downstairs neighbors must get a good shake of the head in the morning. I open the door and traipse up and down those stairs at least twice every morning. *Traipse* is a good word. I plopped into the arm chair and said, "Forget it. I'm not going to make it into work today."

This was much relief to Maggie, who needed to go to the post office later. Errands take on a whole new meaning when you have a baby with you.

In the afternoon, the baby fell into the bottom of the coffee table and it looked like he was going to have his first black eye.

Our Baby Was Born Premature

At 5 p.m., I gave him his bath and changed him into his pajamas. I looked away for a second and when I turned to look at Sean, he was crawling away with a bar of soap lodged in his mouth. Well, he won't do that twice.

Maggie set Sean in his crib for his night time sleep.

He was wailing.

YEAR 2

"Changing the baby's diaper causes the phone to ring."

- Marty Kae Evensen

13 MONTHS

"That's alright, I got what I wanted. I don't need to have sex with you anymore," Maggie said to me as she pushed the stroller down our street.

Maggie was wondering when Sean will be spending time alone during potty time. I want to know when *I* will be spending time alone during potty time.

Last night Sean grew four inches.

This evening I noticed my son pass by an open door. His diaper was around his ankle like a leg warmer. Better fix that before Mags gets home and gives me the "not on my watch" speech.

He's not into me today. I carry him past the TV.
Daddy: No comprende.
Barney: "Oh what's that?"

You want to know one of the best things about having a baby? You have a dance partner.

Had his one-year checkup. Two shots. MMR (measles, mumps, rubella) and Chicken Pox. We are skeptical about taking him for a blood test. If the testing is for lead, we will probably do it—otherwise it seems like too many needles for a baby. It's definitely too many needles for a father. Every time you take the baby into the waiting room after his immunization shots, you tell all the other mothers that it really wasn't that bad.

Being firm and loud doesn't stop the baby from doing what you don't want the baby to do. Directing him into a new task is the answer. It's called misdirection—which he will be doing to us soon.

Sean stuck his head inside his plastic barrel, which holds his rattles, shakers, and vibraphone. He got stuck. I helped him out—but not before videotaping him being stuck.

Sean does this yell that Maggie's mother said is the last thing you want to hear if you're in a car.

He covered his head with a blanket and we pulled it off his face—over and over. It's too bad you lose that joy in later years—unless you're really stoned.

I put a rubber block in my mouth and wouldn't let him pull it out. I saw a father blow up balloons and then fire them into the sky to entertain his two toddlers. At the park, another father yelled and jumped every time his kid put a toy plastic vacuum cleaner near his head. The kid almost passed out from monkey hysterics. It's clear to me; kids love idiots.

Maggie called me and said she was going to leave me because there was pee all over his bed.
A woman at work told me to buy Huggies instead of Pampers.
When I walked in the door at night with my Huggies, Maggie was feeding Sean in the kitchen. There was a pot of ice coffee she had made and she offered me some. Before I could grab the mug she poured some into another cup and said, "Here, I want to make sure you get the one with all the poison in it."

Today he distinctly said, "Kurc, Orp, and Gargoe."

Sean seems to play with his toys upside down and backwards. He's my son. It won't be long before he'll be getting into the backseat by going through the front, driver-side door.

Our neighbor was with her child and husband at a mall. A woman came up to them and asked how old their kid was?
They said, "eighteen months."
The woman shook her head. "Wow, he doesn't look like he's two and a half."
Here's hoping she's not a teacher.

Maggie was with a crying baby all day AND she was on her period. I got home from work. She handed him to me then said, "Why aren't we living in Canada?"
I tried to cheer her up by telling her a joke.
    "How do you spell Canada?"
    "How?"
    "C-eh-N-eh-D-eh."

(the same way he was conceived)   **57**

I'm obsessed with a frozen food for children called *Kid's Cuisine!* It comes in a box. The mascot is KC the Penguin, smiling and pointing to the craziest TV Dinner plate of food ever made. The Kid's Cuisine I picked up was called *Kid's Cuisine, Alien Invasion Pepperoni Pizza.* On the right hand side it says, "HEY! Try more great Kid Cuisine Meals!" Among eight other meals listed are: Confetti Corn Dogs and Jurassic Fried Chicken. KC the Penguin has an antenna coming out of his head. There is lush, cartoon-colored lettering all over the box, filling up the entire cover. A flying saucer is in the bottom left corner with *Parmesan Cheese Meteor Shower* written on it. Apparently, the Parmesan cheese is green. Half way up the left hand side of the box is *Alien Shaped Fruit Snacks.*

Under all this colorful wordage is a picture that sends chills up my back. The meal.

In a blue plastic TV Dinner style tray there is a tiny pizza that looks like they've poured cheese and chunks of bologna (or puke) onto a hockey puck sized piece of dough. Next to it is corn. It's been airbrushed mustard yellow with white painted sparkles on the niblets. You know it's a lot yellower than the actual corn. Then in another tray compartment, you get the Alien Shaped Fruit Snacks.

I flipped the box over. In very small type, the ingredients covered the entire back of the box. There was more typing than a rental car contract.

Enriched wheat flour, bleached wheat flour, malted barley flour, thiamine mono-nitrate, folic acid, water, butter chips, partially hydrogenated soybean oil with artificial flavoring and artificial coloring, dried whole eggs, yeast, starch, sorbitan monosterate, ascorbic acid, dough conditioners, L-cysteine, fungal enzyme, lecithin, dimethyl polysiloxane, propylene glycol added as preservative, TBHQ, calcium propionate, potassium sorbate, pork, beef, salt, spices, seasonings, polysorbate 80, natural smoke flavor, ascorbic acid, citric acid, BHA and BHT, dextrose, cure salt, sodium nitrate propylene glycol, anticaking, FD&C red #3, lactic acid starter culture mozzarella cheese, salt enzymes, cellulose gum, pizza seasoning, sugar, salt, onion powder, cheese powder, dehydrated cheese, buttermilk, maltodextrin, monosodium glutamate, disodium inosinate & guanylate, dehydrated bell peppers, xanthan gum, guar gum, spice extractives, modified enzyme, modified butter fat, sweet whey powder, beta carotene, corn oil, palmitate, corn syrup, sugar, modified food starch, artificial flavors, blue#1, red#41, yellow #5 and 6, beeswax.

In the PARMESAN CHEESE AND COLOR BITS PACKET: basically more sugar.

Under this they listed the NUTRITION FACTS.

It said, "The percent daily values are: Total Fat per serving 20 Grams. Saturated fat 7 Grams. Cholesterol 65 Mg. Sodium 810 Mg. Sugars 22 grams.

Q: What do you get when you have 20 grams of fat and add 22 grams of sugar?

A: Chucky.

On the back of the box there is a space scene and the kids are encouraged to find the "10 hidden aliens in the scene."

It says this meal takes about three minutes in a microwave oven. And that ladies and gentlemen——is radiation.

Ever notice at the zoo the chimps look at the kids like the kids are in the zoo? They don't leave their juice boxes on the ground, either.

I told Maggie I would like Sean to see a zoo, a garden, or a museum at least once a week. I have other ideas that will never see the light of day too.

If a one-year-old baby is up, and it is quiet and peaceful in your home, it means:

1. The baby has made it into the bathroom and is about to drink from the toilet bowl.

2. The baby has discovered a push-pin or tack on the floor and nothing good can come of this.

(the same way he was conceived)   **59**

3. The baby is inside the closet and has unraveled the entire cord from the vacuum cleaner and is sucking on the plug.
4. The baby is inches away from a bowl of cat food on the kitchen floor and the cat's pissed.

After meals sometimes it looks like I've set him down in the middle of a paint ball game.

Tonight, as we hid in our bedroom, he yowl-screeched at us for an hour. I finally peeked into his room and noticed his bottle had fallen out of his crib and was lying on the floor. I crouched down and tippy-toed without being noticed, to the bottle, quickly tossed the bottle back into the crib and dashed out of the room.

He's developed an emergency broadcast test yell: he decided to see how long he could yell before he needed to take a breath. I opened the kitchen door, went down stairs, and around the back of the build-ing to throw some trash into the garbage can. I wanted to see how far a baby's yell would travel. The whole building can hear him.

He figured out how to remove his diaper while wearing a onesie and then took a dump on the hardwood floor. At least this will clean up fairly easy. The cat yacks on the pillow covers; really hard to clean. The good news is—he's smarter than the cat.

15 MONTHS

Maggie gave Sean a pot, a lid, and 2 wooden spoons today. She called me and played Sean's pots and pans solo into my ear. She laughed. "Our poor downstairs neighbor," and then, "Ahh, screw 'em. It's 9 a.m."

Animal magnets and a cookie sheet buys you about ten minutes.

I made some mashed potatoes for Sean and then completely spaced out and put cracked pepper in it. Baby and cracked pepper is a very bad combo plate.

Milk stained clothes that you've misplaced smell like cow chips.

There's a reason you never see a *feng shui* picture-book with a baby in it.

Sean spit up a lot of milk today. He hasn't done that in awhile. I believe it is a reaction to more teeth coming in. At least that's what I'm saying out loud. I know the real reason is because the sippy cup I gave him to drink from today was the one that had been left in a hot car for a week with hot milk in it.

Morning: A garbage truck broke down in the alley right under the dining room/baby room where Sean takes his nap.
Afternoon: Sean flew off the chaise lounge and landed square on top of his head. I believe wrestlers call that move "The Pile Driver?"
Later on, a car alarm went off next to one of the shops in the alley.
Evening: They fixed the garbage truck and it revved away and Sean got up off the rug too fast and slammed his head into the

(the same way he was conceived)   61

corner of the end table. After he stopped crying it seemed like seven or eight ambulances raced by or maybe an ambulance driver was lost and kept circling our block? I made a futile attempt to silence the roar of the city by closing the dining room window.

We can't take him outside unless we put makeup on him.

Finally, around 8 p.m. the baby is asleep and by the looks of him—if a wrecking ball came through the dining room wall right now, he would snore right through it.

Tonight I made a three-block tower out of his rubber blocks and then dissembled them and said, "Now, you try."

Sean picked up the yellow one and placed it on top of the blue one. I clapped, "Yeah, that's it, Sean."

Sean clapped, too.

I made another three-block tower and dissembled it and once again said, "Now, you try."

Sean just clapped.

Maggie came into the kitchen today while I was cooking and Sean sat on the floor looking up at the stove. She said, "Always face the pot handles toward the back of the stove." I thanked her.

The American adult dream is to own a home and the American child's dream is to live in a home that isn't broken.

Babies move around like people on a boat during a storm.

Monday. Memorial day. I took Sean to a nearby park. At least 50 families with at least 50 kids in each family were already there. Everyone was grilling with their own barbecues. Smoke was out of control, and toddlers caterwauled and ran around in circles. They were letting their trash blow away into the park. I found a patch of grass and let Sean crawl around a bit. He went forward about six feet. From behind—a soccer ball shot past us, missing Sean by six inches, and then a teenage kid did the same. I put Sean back into his stroller and headed for the nearest path. Then, out of nowhere, a Frisbee hit the stroller. It's the first time a park has scared me.

May 30th. Sean walked across the room to me kind of like the first man on the moon, and then he did it again for Maggie, laughing most of the way.

I never quite know what to say when I meet a couple and I can't tell if their kid is a boy or a girl. And if they call the child Cammy or Jean it doesn't help.

(the same way he was conceived)

16 MONTHS

This morning an avalanche-size snowball of toilet paper was on the bathroom floor.

Every time people run into us with Sean they always say, "He's getting bigger!"
At which point I tell them, "And I'm getting smaller."

CANADA TRIP AGAIN

An elderly lady was next to me on the plane. The nicest flight attendant ever employed with Air Canada offered her complimentary beverage service. The senior lady said, "Do you have Green tea?"
The friendly attendant said, "No, ma'am—just Red Rose."
The lady said, "Do you have chamomile green tea?"
   "No—just Red Rose, ma'am."
   "Do you have herbal teas?"
The attendant sized her up and politely said—"Would you like some hot water and lemon?"
The lady stared at him and announced, "Give me coke."

There was a crying baby on board. The only thing worse would be if the father cried every time the baby cried. Watch the nicest flight attendant start drinking.

Aboard the ferry that travels back and forth to the island, I realized that these are shark infested waters and most of our relatives can't swim so this is a great place to have a house. I also realized that 9 out of 10 Canadians on the ferry have trays of french fries. These people will stand in line for 20 minutes to get a tray of french-fries and then wash it down with a pastry and a beer. Some five-year-old Canadian kids look like they have been drinking beer since they were two. I asked the guy behind the cash register as he rang up my fries and gravy if they wheel you right into surgery after the meal.

Our Baby Was Born Premature

I fear Sean's teenage years. The gangly stage where their arms and legs grow faster than the rest of their body and they don't really have facial hair, they just have that dirty fuzz. And they wear basketball uniforms wherever they go.

And boob cleavage used to be in—now butt cleavage is in. If I had a sixteen-year old daughter with a tattoo in the small of her back of an arrow pointing down, and she thought showing her thong was fashionable, the first I'd do is—move the family to an island.

I got a first-time homeowner surprise when I drove up to our house. It took two days to cut the grass. It was so long they could have organized elementary school field trips to study the property. "Everyone, bring your jars!"

You know it's a small town when the barber asks you if you've fixed the loose toilet handle in your bathroom.

The sub-trades in town have found out I live in Hollywood (where they make movies!). They are circling my house like wolves looking for meat. A plumber tried to give me an invoice for $82 because he had a 10 minute conversation with me about my basement. I told him on Earth we call that an estimate. A roofer pulled up, looked at the house for under five minutes and said, "$13,000 —hey man, it's been a rough winter." What kind of tradesman is honest about gouging you? I can hardly wait to meet the mayor when taxes are due.

To attract more customers, bar owners in town are applying for a license so families can bring their children into the bar. Excuse me, but I go to a bar to escape my kid. Let's see—liquor, toddlers, and a dart board. That sounds like unhappy hour.

(the same way he was conceived)

My parents flew out from Ontario to see the house. They told me I eat too fast and I told them they eat too loud.

My neighbor's wife came by to drop off some more paint supplies and to help out. Her nine-year-old was driving around on his bike. I saw him ask his mother 31 questions in 30 seconds. She looked at me and sighed. "I swear he didn't say anything until he was six."

There's a breakfast joint down at the Quay that opens at 5 a.m. A fisherman in there told me, "There's been mornings when I've been outside waiting for them to open."
Some other Canadian things we heard in the restaurant...
"Go fuck your hat, eh!"
"The retirement community in Florida—all the women look like they'll never get pregnant and all the men look like they are."
"Caught a one hundred pound Halibut—it was like lifting a piece of plywood off the bottom of a lake."
"You know what they call 30 inches of rain up here? A dry spell."
"In this town, winter is on Tuesday and Spring is on Thursday of the same week."
"A friend of mine has a giant wooden fish above his gate and under that he has the word. F I S H."

I found out that almost the entire North West coast is a rain forest. The Parks and Recreation in British Columbia do not want you to walk off the trail surface, make noise in the forest, or take anything out of it, such as the sea shells my 70-year-old mother wanted. We had a tug of war on the beach until I finally convinced her to "Drop them, Mother!"
She put up quite a fight though.

Exploring the temperate Rain Forest is cool and quiet. A mosaic to peace. I pictured Sean seeing all these forests and beaches one day.

(the same way he was conceived)

17 MONTHS

Late at night. On the other side of our bedroom door we heard his cries. I opened our bedroom door, and there he was—in the HALL! It's official—he knows how to get out of his crib.

He got his first pair of shoes today after going through half a dozen at the store. Sean's feet are as big as mine.

He likes to walk down the sidewalk holding your hand. The first time I tried this I wasn't at all used to it—so I took him for a drag.

Maggie's grandfather believed in "time out" or "behavior modification."
Reward good behavior and don't reward bad behavior. "Pavlovian response," they call it.
The only thing I'm fairly sure about is that kids aren't happy unless you dance while doing slight-of hand coin tricks in front of them all day.

Today he fell forehead-first into the baseboard. Nothing a package of frozen peas couldn't cure.

Sean pulled out a shoe from one of our household piles and pushed it across the rug like a car. Toys for poor people.

We decided to move close to down town Los Angeles. The reason? The new apartment will give the baby way more room. And—we are insane. To sum up the move in a nutshell, I wish my kid was grown up, we only owned foam furniture, and our cats were dead.

No matter what store I take Sean into along Pico Blvd., he always gets strangers to smile at him. Some of these people speak in their own language but it doesn't matter. They speak to him anyway—in a Tortelleria bakery, a Salvadorian papuseria, or a candy/toy store for kids called El Payacito. One place we passed at the corner of Pico and Vermont had a lit-up sign in front of it, "Gran Cruzada! Problemas como: Brujeria, Envidia, Suerte, Insomnio, Nerviosismo, Vicios, Migranas, Odio, Depresion, Pesadillas, Deseos de suicidio." I can't speak a lick of Spanish, but I can tell this is a bad news sign. We stayed away. It had a Tarot-card-I'm-about-to-be-conned feel to it.

Korean stores seem delighted to be doing business. A few blocks from our apartment there's a Jingle Bell Furniture store, a Joy Bank, a Happy Restaurant, and a Yummi Jewelry store.

Every hot summer day, an ice cream truck pulls up along-side the curb on our street with the music "Pop Goes The Weasel" blaring out of speakers. Hoards of kids surround it—and most of them look like the only exercise they get is when they run after the ice cream truck. It's not an ice cream truck. It's a crime scene.

Sean looks at the little girls from our bay window with the same enthusiasm as the kids inside a car at Lion Safari Amusement Park.

If you put a tiny kid on a front lawn pretty soon lots of tiny kids are on your front lawn.

We've met four new parents—and two of the mothers told Maggie they're on Prozac.

(the same way he was conceived)   **69**

Sean's new toys: Maggie's expensive cell phone. The remote control for the expensive TV. Maggie's expensive sunglasses. Why can't he play with the cat's tail?

Came home to see:
My naked kid from behind. Both hands raised. In his right, a plastic bath toy. In his left, a pail. He's standing in front of our living room bay window that looks out to busy Westmorland Ave. Maybe if I did that the ice cream truck would never park here.

I'm not the best handyman. My wife has a parody song she sings every now and then. It is based on the popular kids cartoon, *Bob the Builder*. Most parents know the tune.
My wife's version goes like this, "Knob the Builder. Can't fix anything. Knob the builder. No he can't."

Sean loves binoculars; especially if he's looking through them backwards through the big lenses, not the small ones.

Sometimes your kid lives on nothing but hot dog wieners, ketchup, and sippy cups of juice.

One of Sean's favorite sports is "bend the blinds." We are never getting our deposit back.

Our Baby Was Born Premature

Good LA Driver's Guide
1. The car horn is not used to warn, it is used to punish.
2. A sign reads, NO LEFT TURN BETWEEN 4PM AND 7PM means you turn left between 4 p.m. and 7 p.m.
3. You should never dim the high beams when there are oncoming vehicles.
4. When stopped in a street, do not turn on any directional signals. It's best to give no indication to other drivers what your intentions are.
5. After a collision, the law requires you to speed away.
6. If your destination is next to your house or apartment, drive there.
7. Cell phone conversations come first; not children in a school zone.
8. Listen to thundering music and bob your head instead of looking for signs and signals, or listening to fire engines.
9. Never drive an extra 10 feet to find parking when you can valet.
10. If your car is side-swiped and you lose your passenger door, do not get it repaired. Continue driving, even with the constant dinging sound, while maintaining a pissed-off look.

Throwing a tantrum when a baby throws a tantrum is like swatting a hornet's nest to stop the buzzing.

The baby monitor-antenna is sticking out of the Diaper Champ. A Q-tip is lodged in the stereo earphone jack. A toothbrush is inside the USB port, which obviously doesn't work anymore. I'm afraid to look in the fridge.

My kid hears, "Stand on the curb until the cars pass." But he never hears, "Give me the remote."

(the same way he was conceived)

There is a tiny "common area" in our apartment complex. A place for working-class people to mingle. I took it upon myself to put in sod and make it into a yard. I was figuring how much topper and steer manure to lay down.

Maggie told me, "Throw his diaper in there."

Mom has been putting Sean to bed already half-dressed for the next day (eg., short pants and PJ top). Less time to get going in the morning.

CANADA VACATION (WELL NOT REALLY)

Maggie took Sean to see his grandparents. The one's in Toronto. How I convinced her to get on a plane with a one-and-a-half-year-old and visit my senior parents *and* my drunk cousins is a true Testament to my charisma, ingenuity, and cunning. My wife would call it selfishness.

On day 3 of my bachelorhood—in the middle of an afternoon nap I had a visitation from some kind of demon-force which hovered over my bed. It had a skeletal face and wore a black cloak. I wanted to get up but my arms and legs were rendered useless. I opened my mouth and tried to yell at it but no sound came out. In a cold sweat I went face-to-face with this ghoul-spirit.

I woke up to the sound of the ice cream truck on the street blaring another looped nursery rhyme. I think it was "Welcome To Our World Of Toys."

I have to believe that Maggie wished some kind of Irish Banshee on me all the way from eastern Canada.

I want Sean to have his own orchard. Is that unrealistic?

I was looking at some old holiday cards and Baby cards Maggie keeps in a photo album. I came across one in particular and went about writing a long overdue Baby Thank You Card:

Dear Aunt Connie,

You pruned, weak-minded, intolerant eh-hole. How dare you send me some Hallmark-type card and scrawl a few words on the inside of it, as if you had dinner to prepare and needed to seal it fast. Not a single thought went into that lame card—absolutely no information about anything. Just a hack writer's generic poem. And I quote, "Butterflies and bright colors, sunlight and smiles. That's what a little boy's heart desires."

Wrong. A little boy desires a safe house and eight or nine meals a day. He desires to go to college too. So if you can't help us out with advice or friendship or cash—why bother keeping up appearances? Oh, I almost forgot. You included an Easter card too. Signed, *From Bob and Connie.*

Both names signed by you. You're a lazy faker. I noticed it cost $1.65 to mail it from Canada. Guess that's why you included the Easter card stuffed inside the other card. To save money. Happy Easter, huh. I bet the people in Palestine are having a happy Bunny day as bombs explode and power is shut off in their neighborhoods —ever think of that? Of course not. You're a self-obsessed do-gooder who likes malls. How about pondering deforestation? Water pollution, health care, the arts, anything!?

There's no return address on the envelope. You don't want us to know where you live. I understand.

I hope my mother is annoying you with pictures of my baby like you annoy me with pictures of your kids' babies. They all look the same, by the way.

You know what your problem is? You're afraid of the dark.

Other than that—it's been cool here at night. I prefer it this way. Los Angeles can get so hot.

Love, Paul

(the same way he was conceived)

19 MONTHS

I got the report from Maggie as she returned from her trip to Canada to visit her senior in-laws. And she will be running up my credit card shortly as revenge.

"Grandpa was very impressed by Sean carrying a pair of slippers to his grandma. He said, 'He is going to be the smartest kid in school.'"

Maggie told my dad, "A dog can do that." Maggie also told me, "All grandparents say the same thing about babies, "Eaagh! Watch his head!"

We went to a coworker's house in Riverside, which is in the middle of the desert. If you cracked an egg on the hood of your car it would be done in ten seconds. His in-laws, the "Yellers," showed up with their kids. My ears were actually ringing—as everyone sat and yelled at each other for eight straight hours. The adults yelled back and forth and their kids screeched and ran around in circles with colorful swords in their cloven-hoofed paws. Food was ground into the carpets and stained underwear lay all over the kid's rooms like land mines. A hairless dog was trying to jump up on everything, and I think I saw a cat up on the kitchen counter eating from a bowl of party snacks.

Everybody started slathering each other with bottle after bottle of sickly, sweet smelling suntan lotion. If you want to know what that smells like—go to a porn theater. We all went out to the pool in the backyard, where the noise became amplified. They yelled and yelled and yelled. The pool toys became indoor toys. There was jumping and smashing and thumping and dragging. Every room in this house was piled high with unfinished adult projects, kids garbage, and toys. Toys that were used for about an hour in their natural life and then discarded. Crazy toys—like a huge plastic barbecue that makes the sound of sizzling meat on a grill. Then it was time to eat cake.

These people have a knife in their kitchen that is specially designed to cut square chunks of cake. Who buys a knife that cuts only cake?

"Hmm, you know, Honey—we're going to be eating a lot of cake in this house, so I'm going to buy this cake-cutting knife to speed up all the cutting that we'll be doing."

It was about six in the evening when the yelling reached a peak. I nearly screamed, "My eyes! My eyes!" The father of a two-year-old girl named Lisa was playing video games with three dirty, gangly kids—and the other Yellers were all yelling at each other in the dining room, which was adorned with art you see on the walls at a Denny's restaurant. Suddenly, Maggie raced through the living room as the two-year-old girl came shooting down the staircase headfirst, crying. There was a momentary calm—as everybody watched Maggie holding a sobbing little Lisa who almost broke her neck.

Where was my baby during all of this?

Oh there he was.

Sean had just fallen out of his chair but he didn't cry because he had never had that much cake-icing on his face before, which proved much more interesting than terror.

Toddlers. No matter what they do they could care less if they're naked when they do it.

Another doctor's appointment. We weaved the stroller though the tiny waiting room which was packed like sardines with kids. I looked at all the people waiting and secretly wondered what they were probably wondering about me: "What's wrong with that guy's kid?"

Everybody gets in trouble for being late except doctors. You get to your appointment and they say, "Take a seat, the Doctor will be right with you." What they should say is "Take a seat, the Doctor will be right with you after he goes home and does some yard work."

Guess I'll read *Chatelaine* magazine from cover to cover. I'm never going to make a slow-cooker breakfast. But thanks *Chatelaine*.

Then they finally call you. And they take you into a room and say, "Take a seat, the Doctor will be right with you."

(the same way he was conceived)   75

Only at the doctor's do they have a waiting room inside a waiting room.
And what's up with the scribbling on the prescriptions? Doctors can't write or tell time and I'm trusting them to care for my child. Don't get me wrong, I couldn't face all the sick people every day. Avian flu, duck flu, bird flu, pig flu, whatever happened to good 'ol flu flu? I miss the flu. Mad cow disease, mad chipmunk disease (that's a bad one—apparently you lose your nuts.)
I get it. They quickly scribble anything. Just to get you out of their office.

Most parents don't want their kids to learn what life's about. They want them to learn what their life is about.

Maggie wants to have a family dinner once a week without fail—preferably vegetarian and on Saturdays.
One Week Later: Maggie, Sean, and I went to an all gay (except for us) pool/barbecue party in Pasadena on Saturday evening. We gave Sean whatever burger and hot dog left-overs they had on the grill and then Sean dug through the cooler of champagne and beer bottles that were bobbing around in ice water until someone gave him a juice box.

Who has time to do dishes when you have a baby? The verdict is still out on dishwashers too. You put something in a dishwasher with any dirt on it—you end up with hot dirt.

Our Baby Was Born Premature

There was a huge parade up the street today—baby's first. El Salvadorian Independence Day which brings with it a lot of floats and belly dancers. Ice cream vendors strolled by pumping bicycle horns in their free hands. There were men in cowboy hats carrying cotton candy on long pieces of wood. Every kid on the street was blowing toy horns, and a lot of men were blowing those long, plastic, colored horns that you hear at football games. I hate the sound of that horn—the black sheep of the horn family.

Parade music is always too loud. People who aren't musicians always volunteer at parades.

It worked though—Sean took a nap.

The baby room is almost finished. I'm a pretty good painter. Not art. House. I bought a 3-D solar system kit from a store called Imaginarium. It comes with 1,000 decals of glow in the dark stars and I stuck every single one up on his ceiling. Music and visual art have got to have a subconscious affect on him for the better. If he ends up in jail, I was wrong.

Sean was at the park today. He traded his bulldozer for another kid's lawn mower.

Sean discovered a bag of potato chips on a display rack in line at the supermarket. They always have that last minute display rack of poison to get a few more bucks out of you.

"It's a good thing they reminded me of the dill pickle potato chips and Yoda Pez dispensers. What was I thinking—thank you super-market."

Just before I escaped, Sean pummeled the chip bag like he was making pizza dough and I had to buy something else I didn't intend to buy.

(the same way he was conceived)   77

Maggie was looking at a web site called BabyBibz.com. Dozens of beautiful designs for bibs: Ralph Lauren, autumn flowers flannel, vintage trucks flannel. A website for rich people buying designer garments for spit.

A young father with two boys, one two- and one six-months-old, pushed his double-stroller up to the counter at Rexell Drug Mart, held up a pack of condoms and said, "Well, let's see if this brand works?"

No matter how dry it is everywhere else—kids always go right to the puddle.

20 MONTHS

It is astonishing how much noise a baby can get through that one inch space at the bottom of a closed door.

A year-and-a-half-year-old's falling-down-on-the-floor-tantrum over the amount of milk in a sippy cup; where else can one experience this kind of behavior? Oh yeah, parents at a hockey rink.

Sean ate his spaghetti noodles much like an owl would dissect a field mouse. It was on the table, on the chair, on the floor—a tail coming out of his mouth—cheese. Let's try to forget.

He actually bit Maggie the other night when she was trying to put him to sleep.
There's always advice; my mother who just turned 70 said, "Bite him back."
Maggie's mother from the hippie generation said, "Throw water on him."

We settled on a book recommended by some fellow new-moms. The book is by some guy named Ferber. In it, he has a 5, 10 and 15 minute rule. The idea is to put the baby down and leave the room. The kid throws a tantrum. You use a stop-watch and wait 5 minutes. Then you go into the bedroom and comfort the child. You put him down to bed and leave the room—again. This time for 10 minutes, etc. His tear glistened face fell asleep in a small puddle on the floor near the door after 45 minutes of this.

Q: What is louder than trying to find the right pot in a kitchen cupboard of pots and pans?
A: A *baby* trying to find the right pot in a kitchen cupboard of pots and pans.

(the same way he was conceived)   79

Sean stood in front of the hall mirror, naked, and said, "Pee." And did exactly that.

Morning. All's quiet. A few birds are waking up. I open Sean's bedroom door to see him. The light in the room is gray and feels morning-moist. He has just climbed out of his crib and is lying on a blanket on the floor by his crib. He sees me. Smiles. He yawns, stands up, and very softly says something impossible to understand.

Then he jumps into my arms. He is wearing blue PJ pants with a cockroach and huge beetle pattern on them. The PJ top is red with a ladybug on it, and he has on red socks.

I think to myself, *This is a love I have never experienced before*. And trying to hug them while they are running is hard because they have more important things to do—like falling down laughing after eating a purple crayon.

Sean hit Jacob on the head with a plastic flute—effectively ending their play date.

We found this video called *Baby Mozart*, and he seems to be amused by it. Mozart's music plays under scenes of vintage toys in use. The producers of the vid claim that babies exposed to Mozart did better on intelligence and spatial testing than other kids exposed to other composers.

I guess it works—after watching half of the video Sean somehow figured out how to log into PayPal spend $100 and then disconnect the modem.

Tuesday morning. I started out the day at Starbucks trying to pour cream into my coffee cup which had the lid on it. I left my cell phone at home and drove back 10 city blocks to retrieve it. Sean was up now. I really wanted to escape without him seeing me but it was too late. He kept me there until I was hours late for work. You can "call in sick," but it's tricky to call in because you're watching Elmo.

I'm pushing Sean through an aisle of canned goods at the market. He lets out a short squeal. Somewhere in the store—maybe five aisles away—another baby squeals, and then a third baby at the front of the store yelps.
Babies communicate like dogs in a neighborhood at night.
I had to give him a banana to stop the extra-terrestrial-baby-talk thing going on.
I figured, "I'll worry about the peel when I get to the cash register."

I entered the kitchen to see the baby climb into the dishwasher and come out holding a steak knife. I screamed like Janet Leigh in *Psycho*.

21 MONTHS

Five rolls of colored tape can keep a kid busy for an hour. The cleanup is just as much fun because they get to make a "tape ball." These colored tapes are great toys and you don't have to buy them if you have access to the copy room at work.

There is one city park close by in our L.A. hood. There are always two or three homeless people there and one thing's for sure—they're not playing. There is graffiti on the play equipment. I guess graffiti's okay—if there wasn't any graffiti, the hookers wouldn't know where to stand. The palm trees are spray painted too and smell like urine.
All this means—I put Sean in the car and drive across town to West Hollywood Park. An hour in traffic, I get there and find out they allow dogs on the property.

All moms at playgrounds carry the same rations. Sippy cups and Goldfish crackers.
All moms but not the single dad in charge of two kids who is wearing a back pack and has become dehydrated. The kind of guy that has tantrums and makes a child with special needs cry because that child was on a swing too long while his kids are waiting.

Sean and Jacob are best friends even though we live in different neighborhoods now. Maggie and Jacob's mother were amazed that they could actually read a magazine while the two boys played together.

Our Baby Was Born Premature

Since the holiday season is upon us we have been getting the usual barrage of mail order magazines. *Back to Basics Toys* showed up today. They say they are committed to providing families with a traditional, high-quality play experience. On page 25, they have what they call "authentic bagpipes in a junior size." There's a picture with an instruction booklet and they describe the toy as such: "Terrific to march with, these kid-tailored bagpipes look sharp anywhere and reward the enthusiastic player with a genuine sound!" So. if you want to get back at a parent it is the perfect gift.

Babies love steering wheels even if it's not steering anything.

Maggie made black-out curtains for baby's room in cool, vintage patterns. We've been in parent's homes that have towels on their kid's windows, desperately trying to ensure nap time. Two-year-olds are like short vampires.

One of his new words is "Ta-ta." He says this instead of "good-bye." He waves and says, "Ta-ta." We have no idea where he picked it up. Today, he was eating a hot dog. He held each piece out before eating it and said, "Ta-ta," and then ate it. He continued this until the wiener was gone.

As I climbed the stairs of the apartment after returning home from work I was thinking, "It's quite exciting to anticipate Sean's unique and emerging abilities."
I walked in the door—he ran to me, hugged me, and then showed me how he tumbles around on the rug. Good enough.

(the same way he was conceived)

He knows how to say, "Coo-kay." Worse, he knows what a "Coo-kay" is.

Sean mimics a lot. Mommy made a smooching sound and he started imitating her and then walked over and planted one on her mouth. This never works for guys at the park watching the girls go by.

I read this book about quirky kids. In it they list all the aberrant behavior seen in children. They judge whether the child is getting the "gestalt" and not missing what's going on around them. If they aren't getting the gestalt—then it could be considered Right Hemisphere Dysfunction.
Pragmatic Language Disorder. They say this is when a child waxes eloquent about their area of special interest but they may not be able to stop, and they interrupt without regard for who's talking.
Another behavior problem for children in the book is Speech and Language Delay. Problems with give and take in conversation.
Motor Delay. The child demonstrates clumsiness, unsteadiness.
Anxiety Disorder. This is when a child reacts out of proportion from a real threat.
The quirky kids book goes on and on about things to watch for in your child: Separation Anxiety Disorder, Obsessive Compulsive Disorder, Attention Deficit Disorder, Oppositional Defiant Disorder, Tourettes Syndrome.
This book *sounds like everybody I know.*

Toddlers force cats to higher ground. "A shelf, the bed—anywhere the *Thing* can't get me."

Today I'm going to translate all the yelling and convert it to peace and harmony. I am Gandhi Dad.

Noon: Sean broke a glass and then started to pick up the broken pieces. Gandhi Dad turned into Sailor Dad. Sean constantly reminds me to rework my plans.

The holidays are upon us and this means no tree and no ornaments. Nothing can go up in our apartment without Sean ripping it apart immediately, and whatever he doesn't pull down—the cats will.

One city block to a baby is a mile to a parent.

Sean and I went out for a walk in the hood. We passed a guy who's sweating and shrieking on the corner about the rapture coming and headed across to a ditch because Sean was more interested in dandelions.

Every couple wanting a baby needs to have a lecture on the meaning of tired. It's a washed ashore tired. A tired that our friend Joan, who has two under the age of two, told us about.

"There are days when I've stood at the kitchen sink with the water running so my kids won't hear me crying."

I hope he's smart, but to a point. I don't want him to play concert piano at five. It's just weird to see a five year old in a tux bowing.

We were invited to our first "lighting the Menorah" ceremony. It marks the beginning of Chanukah. The Menorah was lit and our friend started to read an old story, and at that exact moment Sean started blowing out the candles. Our friend's kid followed. They snuffed seven out of eight.

(the same way he was conceived) 85

CHRISTMAS AT MY IN-LAWS

We decided to get the family in the car and drive on a freeway for eight hours all the way to another city to see Maggie's family at Christmas. The reason we did this is because we have not yet gained the wisdom of the elders ...
"Let thy younger and dumber come to you."

At the first gas station on the I-5 freeway, I saw a commando couple in their tank sized Ram van packed to the windows with children, toys, luggage, bicycles, kayak rack, and video screens installed behind the seats. The tires on their truck where as tall as the average nine-year-old boy. I say the more expensive the wedding the quicker the divorce.

Trying to sleep in the same bed as a baby is like preparing to be attacked by wild animals—never leave any food out and protect your eyes and belly.

Grandpa Michael and Grandma Becky fastened a metal gate (which looked like something from a kennel) to prevent him from entering the kitchen. Sean white-knuckled the fence and started shaking it like a kid at a canceled Foo Fighters concert.

The family is trying to get used to climbing over the metal kitchen gate when they need food or drink (which is every five minutes at Christmas.)
"Hey Ma, you might want to put some underwear on under that robe."

Our Baby Was Born Premature

He cried blobby tears when Maggie and her sister left to go to town but stopped short of throwing himself on the floor. He didn't get that gene.

It is Christmas in this house and it brings stories of Christmas past . . . such as the time Grandpa Michael assembled balsa wood planes for the kids and inadvertently sliced the tip of his finger off with a knife. He still managed to wrap the gifts though. The following morning, the kids were pretty much disappointed with the planes and couldn't figure out why the wrapping paper had blood on it.

Sean was scooped up and carried to the bedroom for his afternoon nap. He did that cry all kids do, where they make it seem like they've lost all their oxygen, like they're sucking to a full stop. Gea-huh, geh-huh, geh-huh . . . they hold the last geh-breath for a few seconds and then let you have it with another teary squawk. All the adults laugh.

Another thing babies are good for—they remind you to put things away.

My brother-in-law, Mike, told me when they were kids his mother was walking down a street with his brother, Dave. She said, "Where did you get that gum you're chewing?"
Dave said, "It's everywhere!"
He had found the gum on the sidewalk.

If you're listening to the Grateful Dead on Christmas, you're probably in California.

(the same way he was conceived)   **87**

My mother in Canada sent her annual parcel of Christmas presents. Among them, a tooth brush (how *Grandma* is that?)

Maggie's family didn't have a lot of money when she was growing up. She remembered a conversation she had with her dad at Christmas.
"Did you hear the reindeer on the roof, Dad?"
"No—those are rats."

Babies love sticks or empty wrapping paper tubes. It gives them a sense of great power.

I woke up from a "30-minute-before-travel" nap. I was still in that time between sleep and awake—still thinking about the dream that woke me up. It had turtles in it. And there were all kinds of entrances and exits. I've always been apprehensive of entrances because I know it means an exit is coming. We put ourselves through a calculated fatigue that drapes us in unspeakable sorrow, Christmas after Christmas, as we constantly enter and exit—always heartbroken. We're like those tiny just born turtles frantically crawling across rocks and sand toward the ocean tide. If they don't get picked off by a seagull, they get swept up in a blanket of sea foam and cast out by the winds and the moon to meet their fate among the bigger fish, barely conscious that there's a horizon out there at all. And those are the lucky ones. Merry Christmas everybody.

On the drive back we got caught in what seemed like a tornado on the narrow San Raphael bridge, with transport trucks passing us on either side. I've never seen rain like this. God-like rain. We pulled over in Berkeley and called a hotel from a gas station. It is one of the oldest hotels in Berkeley. Sean didn't care much for the grand lobby or the ornate chandeliers or the spa. He loved riding on the Bellman's luggage cart, though.

Our Baby Was Born Premature

23 MONTHS

All parents of toddlers celebrate New Year's Eve by going to bed at 8:30 p.m.

While I'm driving I like to stretch one arm behind me and attack my kid's leg while he's in his car seat. It is tradition; my father used to do this to me. Sometimes I reach back with scraps of food too. Little fingers grab the piece of food—and then I hear rustling. He has the hands of a Raccoon. They work particularly well with those miniature tangelos.

I'm reading this book, *Father-Son Healing: An Adult Son's Guide* by Dr. Joseph Ilardo. In it he says, "By seeing how his father reacts to failure or disappointment the son learns the way a man is supposed to respond."
No wonder Sean yells and cries like a baby.

Sean was scared of his shadow today; all the way across the park.

They're not nannies, they're drug dealers. When the kids act up, they just give them suckers. I see how they work it at the park. The kids all have purple and yellow mouths and turn into Gremlins with bad hair. And what's up with strangers offering your kid candy as if it's a good thing? Even grandpas and grandmas? The barber shop, the doctor. Everyone is terrified of a crying kid.

More found food. This time an oatmeal cookie from the ground. Had to use my finger to get it out of his mouth.

Sean was drawing on a piece of paper with his crayons in his room, and I heard snapping and then spitting.

(the same way he was conceived)

24 MONTHS

They say possession is $^9/_{10}$ of the law. You may own a building, but if you have tenants, it's not really *your* building. I look at it this way: once someone shits somewhere it's pretty much theirs.
"Okay, man—you can have the pillow."

Q: What adheres to a surface better than Krazy glue?
A: Raisin Bran.

He really is small. If you have to hold a banana under one arm in order to hold a phone with two hands—you are small.

There is no such thing as good looking puke. Why is there always pizza in it? If you drank a case of Evian water then puked, there'd be a pepperoni in there.

Sean turned two-years-old today. Eight kids showed up with their moms. Charlotte, Heather, James, Jacob, Daniel, Ethan, Francis, and some kid named Jocass, or something I can't remember. Halfway through the loudest party ever—everything became unearthly quiet. A holy feeling. I came down the hall and turned into the dining room and THERE IT WAS ... all the kids were eating cup-cakes.
A couple of moms asked for coffee. Maggie had a pot on. She had bagels, pastries. They were clutching their cups of coffee close to them and humming.
"Oh, thank you," they said.

"Paul, your two-year-old son hasn't had anything for breakfast. Do you seriously think it's a good idea to squirt whipped cream into his hand?"

90

YEAR 3

"Trying to clean your house while your children are growing is like shoveling the walk while it's snowing."

— Phyllis Diller

25 MONTHS

He ate his broccoli last night, and it was nice to see him finish up all his meatballs while wearing a toy fireman's hat.

Until I had a kid I had never seen so many crackers. There are boxes with every kind of cracker imaginable in our cupboards, in my bed, in the glove box of the car with a Hot Wheels car. The chenille covered sofa looks like a seagull dump.

Freed two-year-olds at a mall act like the ball in a pinball game. And they yell at everything they see.

I have taken to finishing up scraps from my kid's plate because food is expensive; pancake leftovers, broccoli on the floor. I'm like a crazy dog, or something. Let's hope I don't start eating my own shit.

Maggie said, "You never wanted a family dog because of your no pet dog rule—turns out you just wanted all the leftovers for yourself."

My downstairs neighbor has at least 50 cousins living in his apartment, and they all choose to park their cars in front of my garage so I can't get my car out in the morning. I get them back by bouncing a basketball in my living room at odd hours until they bang on their ceiling with a broom.

Our Baby Was Born Premature

There is a kids basketball hoop about five feet off the ground on the court at the Santa Monica park; an hour away in traffic unless there're police barricades because another fugitive's on the loose. He has developed his own style for shooting hoop. I lift him up by clutching him under his arms so his legs are dangling, and he dumps the ball in the hoop.

I'm pretty sure not even NASA engineers can figure out how to fasten and secure child car seats.

(the same way he was conceived)

26 MONTHS

I never thought having a toddler boy would mean I would learn all about the fire department. I'll see a fire truck parked on a street and I pull over. One time a fireman gave Sean a tour. I know where all the tools are kept, such as the pick ax, hydraulic door opener, and jaws of life. I know the difference between a pumper truck and a toxic chemical engine, and I know if Sean puts on a real fire hat he will fall over.

Maybe it's because I'm from Canada, but I don't always lock our car doors. This infuriates Maggie. She called me at work—and peeled me, "Why did you leave the car door open?!"
I asked her what she was referring to?
She said I left the car door open a few days ago and she was just remembering it and it made her mad.

I went to a toy store and bought a small plastic fire engine—because eleven of them aren't enough.

My toddler loves to sit at the dinner table and watch his milk go everywhere except his mouth. My cat gave up his position as alpha male in the house ... the day he realized that "Indeed, sometimes milk rains from the sky."

Sean dragged Mommy's bra into the living room today. It could have been worse; a vibrator could have showed up in front of company.

Decided to take Sean to an art gallery. Not for the art—for the grass. There are all kinds of gardens and grassy areas surrounding the gallery. There is no grass where I live so my travels to find a lawn in L.A. continue.

He was playing around the statues of various art benefactors nobody ever looks at when a young woman gave us an extra ticket for one of the exhibits.

It was the Diane Arbus photography exhibit called *Revelations*.

She is famous for her black and white stills in the fifties and sixties —where everyone has a morbidly confused look on their face.

Perfect for a toddler.

Inside the gallery it was quite busy. Sean discovered that there are places big people go where it's important to be quiet. In one of the rooms, Sean stood in the corner and put his finger up to his lips to passers-by and went, "Shhhh."

I really enjoyed taking him to the gallery. We even saw one of Arbus's cameras. A Rolleflex. I bet she never imagined her pictures would help teach a toddler how to behave.

We ventured into another gallery at the museum where there were exquisite two-hundred-year-old paintings in large, cavernous rooms. But Sean's favorite exhibit was the contemporary water fountain.

In one of the rooms he started to walk backwards and said, "Beep beep beep beep," just like the trucks he's heard. A guard came running into the room to witness a two year old going in reverse toward a statue of Buddha.

This morning I got into the car. Closed the door. Turned on the ignition. The windshield wipers sprung on, the hazard lights started flashing, and the AC fan was blasting on the highest setting. I found coins from the change tray all over the floor mats, too. At least he hasn't figured out how to release the hand break yet.

(the same way he was conceived)   95

Where do you go to find music a toddler will like? I went to the Salvation Army. It makes for a great afternoon to browse the bins, looking through the old 33 rpm vinyl kids records. They are usually a quarter a piece. But after you go home and make a compilation of the best tracks onto a tape that you can play in your car, and you see how it affects your kid in the back seat, they become priceless.

Most newly released celebrity toddler nursery rhyme CDs suck. The same songs are on every CD. But going retro and making No Rage Mix Tapes on cassette is a great hobby.

But toddlers favorite sounds by far are still the belching and farting sound effects.

How can a shoe that's two inches long cost $69.00?

Sean tore the curtains from the windows in the living room. Maggie stopped in her tracks—quite mad.

"Sean Robin—(you know when you get the middle name your parents are mad) did you tear down those curtains!"

He looked at Maggie and said, "All gone. Bye, bye."

27 MONTHS

Toddlers find sugar. They are like Komodo Dragons (it is said they can smell a dead animal from five miles away.)
Once you've used the words 'Dairy Queen Blizzard Shake,' they will repeat these words until you are broken.

CANADIAN ROAD TRIP

We decided to rent out our house in Canada. A family trip is in order—we're driving up there.
We bought some rubber boots for Sean, anticipating rainy season in Vancouver, Canada. He seemed to get into them easily. Then he grabbed hold of the garden hose and filled each boot with water.

Vancouver. You know you're in Canada because the bugs are bigger. I'm pretty sure I saw a horsefly with a jockey on it.
We gave my sister-in-law Rachel a call and asked if her house was baby-proofed?
She said, "No."
Maggie said to me, "Well, it will be when we leave."

Sean got used to Aunt Rachel's bedroom for his afternoon nap by sobbing at the closed door. I did the 5, 10, 15 minute Ferber method thing, getting all the way to 15 minutes. He finally stopped wailing, so I snuck away. But then a few minutes later, I heard a strange sawing sound. I went back downstairs and slowly pushed open Rachel's bedroom door. Sean was wedged against it like a door stop. He was snoring on top of one of Rachel's bras. I lifted him up and put him into bed. One side of his head was entirely covered in tears and snot.
He was out cold. Guess he likes bras.

(the same way he was conceived)

Showed up at the house on Vancouver Island and wondered about a local phenomenon.

Motor homes. They're everywhere. The Canadian dream is to have a house on a lake. I saw a motor home with a small pool in the roof. The Most Desperate Guy Looking for the Canadian Dream Award——goes to him.

Had to come to a full stop on Beaver Creek Rd. as two pigs trotted madly across the road and then into the bush, followed shortly after by a man wearing a bloodied apron and carrying a long knife. Wow. That can't be FDA approved.

Maggie hung our laundry on the clothesline. It was just beautiful out. Not a cloud anywhere. It was the first time we'd ever done that. Our neighbor Al said, "You guys hang'n' out your laundry like in Los Angeles?"

Maggie said, "In L.A., if you hang your clothes on the line, it's the last time you'll see your clothes."

At breakfast, Sean poured cream into his apple juice and it curdled, of course. Then he drank it.

My next-door neighbor has one leg. Sometimes he takes it off when he's puttering around in his garden or around his car.

A few weeks ago in Los Angeles, Sean took an elderly woman's cane and walked away with it. Maggie had to retrieve it and return it to the stranded woman.

Today, he went for the neighbor's fake leg that was leaning against the car. Maggie ran over, "No, no, no, no, Sean!"

I guess kids have the right idea about disabled people. They treat them like everybody else.

Two-year-olds act a lot like drunks.

"Hiiiiiii!"

"Bye, bye truck."

"Bye, bye car."

"Uh oh."

They spill their crackers in order to eat them.

They throw up, pass out on the floor, and you have to carry them to bed.

It was time to work on the upstairs bathroom floor. It had 50-year-old green tiles that were peeling up here and there. We met a fellow who rides around town on a mountain bike and carries tools in a backpack. He lives in the homes he repairs and trades work for rent. He told me what to buy and came by a few days later to lay down new linoleum. The first thing he did was remove the world's oldest vanity. He tipped the trap upside down and said, "Too bad—no wedding rings."

Then he removed the toilet. Under it—a case of nasty. He took out his putty knife and started scraping up what had caked under the toilet and said, "This is the stuff you make sandwiches with."

The ceiling in the bathroom is slanted dramatically. It's not really a bathroom; it's more of a crouching area where you can go to the bathroom. Anywho—he stood up too fast and then said, "Yup—the ceiling's still there."

This man finished the job with no supplies left over except a handful of nails. He was a pro.

I'm not a pro carpenter. I'll show up to a construction site with a crayon behind my ear and an Easter basket full of candy, "Hey guys, is this the load bearing wall? I'll take that down first."

(the same way he was conceived)   **99**

Carpentry math is different than any other kind of math. I know how to measure my erection. I've done that a few times. It's 6 $^3/_{16}$ inches long. That I know.

When I finish assembling a plumbing job—there's always one part remaining. That's never good.

As for basic household wiring ... there's a saying: "You never want to hire an electrician with singed eyebrows."
That's me. But my favorite carpentry line has got to be, "Try your best and caulk the rest."

While we were ripping wallpaper down and painting, a few people came by to inquire about renting the house.
What Not To Say To A Prospective Landlord
1. We have four kids, a dog, and a cat. My husband's on disability. He has rods in his back because a branch fell on his head.
2. I only need the top floor. Looking around 200 a month.
3. I have a bunch of lathes and saws I need to hook up. Can you show me your electric panel?

A mill town comes with industrial accidents. My next-door neighbor has one leg. Lost in a tree falling accident. The guy next to him has no legs because of diabetes, and the house a couple down from ours in the other direction has a guy on a leash in the backyard. I don't even want to get into that.

When you have a toddler you never have a complete set of cutlery. That's why families get dogs. To find the fork in the garden.

Our Baby Was Born Premature

On our last morning in Canada, we sat on the front porch looking at snow capped Mt. Arrowsmith in the not-too-far distance.
Maggie said wishfully, "You can take a Greyhound back to L.A. I'm staying."

You know you're in the U.S.A. when you look at a restaurant menu. They are always bigger. And then there was the Kids Menu.
Fluffer Nutter French Toast (Marshmallows melted in-between frosted bread with a side of syrup).
Corn Doggies (Deep battered sweetened cake around wieners).
Nachos (hot, melted, sugary, orange cheese poured over a pile of salt).

Somewhere driving through Washington we are jarred by the sound of a huge bird-dropping splattering against something. I actually jumped in my seat.
After coming to my senses I realized it was a quarter of a banana hitting the dash board, hurled with precision from a small parent hunter in the back seat.

In another hotel room. Sean goes into the bathroom with an empty cup. There's some banging around, and just before I jumped up off the bed, his mom said, "If he can't get it out of the sink you know where he's going to get his water."

We decided to stop in Nevada City California to see Sean's great grandmother and grandfather (who he's never seen).
The only thing I remember is the button that Sean's grandfather had pinned to his cowboy hat: "Everything I need to know about life I learned by killing smart people and eating their brains."
We are almost back in Los Angeles.

(the same way he was conceived)   101

28 MONTHS

Showed up to our neighbor's birthday party for Daniel, who turned one. Sean got onto a plastic lawn mower/car and peddled about zero to sixty in two seconds. The only thing in his path was a little boy named Francis. It's as if time stood still and everyone at the party watched in disbelief—and then it happened. Sean slammed on the brakes and came to a full stop about an inch in front of Francis. Applause.

On my way to a park I decided to take him to a street that was under construction instead; lots of steam shovels, cranes, and bull-dozers. To a two-year-old boy the only thing more fun than dino-saurs is a road under construction.

At the farmers market in Hollywood a woman beside me suddenly got a helping hand with a tomato. She said, "Thank you!"
At the next vendor, while I was buying some peaches, Sean shop-lifted an apple.
It was a good morning.

My two-year-old and I do the dishes 50-50. He dries them and I sweep them up.

Maggie gave me some advice in the kitchen last night.
"If you ever lose your glasses or your keys—check the trash can."

I took him to the downtown central library. He yelled at the ceiling, threw around some stuffed animals that are part of the children's room (Maggie said the animals were probably full of lice), then rolled around on the carpet in a circle. He also went to various bookshelves and carefully selected then removed the metal bookends that hold the stacks in line.

A woman, 60ish, sat and watched all this with a glum expression, mixed with pity.

Sean burst into our bedroom like a cowboy through an old saloon door. He was crying. He stood beside the bed just out of arms reach (on purpose) and cried. Mommy finally got up and made him toast.

Kids love car washes. And it's cheaper than Disneyland. When I put the vacuum cleaner on his pant leg. Cackles.

I parked the car and pushed Sean to the corner of Santa Monica Blvd. and Crescent Heights. The beginning of the Gay Pride parade. He was mesmerized by the "Just Married" float. Men dressed in Bridal gowns singing Madonna's "Like a Virgin." A cannon shot out colorful streamers at the end of the song. He also watched the Sisters of Perpetual Indulgence, fire engines, men with whips, clowns—including the mayor of Los Angeles—and many other floats with people wearing very strange hats (a woman had a three-decker hat made of flowers).

I've been back in Los Angeles a month since our Canada trip—and I feel like if I went to a mind reader I'd get a complimentary pass.

I came home, opened the front door, and Sean greeted me. He was wearing nothing but green rubber boots, diapers and some stickers on his forehead.

(the same way he was conceived)

29 MONTHS

6 a.m. Sean started his day by blowing on his kazoo approximately three inches from my sleeping face.

Here's something I said today, "One of the good things about the terrible twos is it prevents extramarital affairs. The mother is too tired." I never learn that this kind of remark always results in Maggie on a shopping spree with our credit card.

Maggie called to let me know Sean found my deodorant stick in the bathroom, so now he smells like a man.

Walked in the door tonight and found the neighbor's kids and Sean jumping up and down in the living room, clutching apple juice boxes. They had taken all the pillows off the furniture and were hopping onto each one like they were lily pads. The pillows I just had dry-cleaned.

30 MONTHS

Little kids read toy catalogs like grandpas read newspapers.

My sunglasses are MIA. Inside the case for my glasses there are half-eaten crackers.

Sean officially ended his day by repeatedly sticking an orange Tinker Toy pole into Mommy's butt and saying, "Sorry."

How Sean plays Hide and Seek.
First, he covers his eyes, then he faces the corner, and then he says, "Three, four. Three, four. Three, four."

He emptied a huge tub of toys onto the floor, raised his arms over his head and said, "Ta da." Just before company arrived.

(the same way he was conceived)

31 MONTHS

I am flying to Canada with Sean to visit his grandparents. Daddy on a plane with a two-and-a-half-year-old. Before heading to the airport, we make a U-turn and shoot into a craft store. Sticker books. Silly Putty. A picture book of bugs. A felt board with felt adhesive ghosts and half moons, and rolls of colored tape.

My seat assignment was 3D, which sucked because my tray table was farther away than it appeared.

A couple hours into the four-hour flight, the window and seat-back in front of him is covered in tape. It's working.

Only one hour to go and I'm down to my last roll.

At my parents house I changed his diaper on the bathroom floor. Asked my dad, 81, "Do you want in on this action?!" He moaned from the kitchen, "No way."
Apparently his generation of fathers never changed diapers.
My mother commented with a voice the temperature of ice, "He did nothing. "

Sean refused to eat anything at the table tonight. I tried reverse psychology.
"Sean please don't eat any of your peas, thanks.
Amazingly he started shoveling peas into his mouth with both hands.
"Sean whatever you do don't eat that carrot."
Behold! He ate the carrot.
They're such shits.

Our Baby Was Born Premature

The Canadian trip ended too soon and Sean and I were buddies for five hours on a plane going back to Los Angeles. Thank God for in-flight movies. We sat in coach. You know you're in coach when the pilot comes on and says, "Ladies and gentleman I hope you enjoy your flight with us today. First-class passengers will have warm towels to freshen up during your flight. Those of you in Coach section—please feel free to lick the person beside you."

(the same way he was conceived)

32 MONTHS

In Los Angeles, a porta-potty under a cloverleaf freeway interchange is renting for $2,000 a month. If you want the luxury model with the half moon cut in the door—$3,000.

We are moving to Redondo Beach. A little south of Cigarette Butt Beach and Beer Can Cove. And the only reason we are getting our deposit back is because we had a lawyer friend send the request on her stationery. There will not be a lump in my throat saying good-bye to the graffiti covered taco truck permanently parked in front of my apartment.

There is West Coast Time and East Coast Time, and then there is Toddler Time. Traveling two blocks can take 45 minutes.

Kids mean you need more space. You have to throw stuff out. It's hard. I threw out a hockey puck I have been carrying around for 30 years. As I was throwing it into the trash I thought, "Maybe I should put it on Ebay—then I could stay in touch with the buyer and check *in* on my hockey puck every six months."

I have been talking like Sean to Sean, which I know is wrong but I can't help it. So I have been saying things to him like "Pleeth" and "yeth" and "you're welp," which is how he says "you're welcome."

Ten minutes into his nap I saw a tiny hand feeling under the bottom of his bedroom door.
Then a "boing" sound. Over and over. Boing, boing, boing.
He found the door stop.

"Sean, when Mommy and Daddy tell you that we love you it doesn't mean that you can be the ruler of the universe."

Game.
I put on Sean's five-finger-frog-puppet-washcloth. Each finger has the face of a little frog. Then I make a fist. Sean is in the tub—eager. I uncurl one finger and sing very low, "Sean."
Every finger after that gets a higher "Sean," until the last finger —which sings COMPLETELY OFF KEY.
This delights him which delights me because laughter in a bathtub has superior acoustics.

Every time Sean wakes up from a nap he's learned new words. He rarely says them in the correct order though.
"What's that is?"

There are those days when I have to put him into his car seat the same way a cop puts a perpetrator into a squad car; arms behind the back, handcuffed—and then pushing the top of his head down until he's sitting.

Sometimes he brushes his teeth and sometimes he washes his teeth. He does a sound effect of the toothbrush and stands on the toilet seat (because that's the only way he can look in the mirror.) He holds up his brush and goes, "Orrrrrrr."
I don't think he's cleaning any teeth. I'm too tired to care.

(the same way he was conceived)

33 MONTHS

"Did Sean eat the baby carrots I bought for his lunches?"
I noticed there were baby carrots stuffed into his plastic shark on the ledge of the bathtub.
"Never mind."

At the mall, Sean was hunched forward in the first engine car of a train the mall had set up, white-knuckling the horn as the car went around the track. He was yelling at the boy next to him to push the button that controlled the bell.
The noisy train finally stopped and another mom told me as she unstrapped her kid to get him out of his seat, "Be careful not to bump their head on the train roof."
I said, "Thanks," and then lifted Sean right into the train roof.

There was a reason the new fabric softener from Walmart was on close-out. It makes Sean's pajamas smell like vomit.

I can't think of anything that makes me more sick than watching someone picking their nose and eating it. It's worse than cutting yourself and drinking your own blood.

Our Baby Was Born Premature

34 MONTHS

I witnessed Sean having a seizure. It was terrifying and resulted in a siren/ambulance ride to the ER and a dose of Tylenol to bring his 104 temperature down to 98ish. On the ride home Sean saw a police car race past us with full on siren and he yelled, "Can we do it, again! Can we do it, again!"

The day after the seizure Sean started the day by making sure he slammed every single door in the house including cupboards.

Ivares = underwear.

Sometimes toddlers go on nonsense rants. Kind of like a senator on a filibuster.

I happened to see a closed book I'd been reading which had gone from the mantel to the bed. Mom laughed, "Sean threw away your book mark."

I wandered over to the park with the kid and came back an hour later. It was then I realized my slippers were still on, my hair was quite a mess, and my fly was open. No wonder no kids played with us.

Sean's third Christmas came and went without much fuss. At dinner he grabbed hold of some candles that came with wicks joining two together and used them as nun-chucks.

6:30 a.m.
"Keytoe barse on da cows" = "The cat barfed on the couch."

(the same way he was conceived)   III

35 MONTHS

Maggie has been calling me at work in the morning around the time Sean gets up—to share her pain. It always sounds like she's calling from a pet store full of parrots.

I've been trying to do some handyman work around the house. I stare at pieces of wood not yet fastened together thinking, "How do I fix this?" And then the thought, "How about a match?"
I hung a door and almost hung myself. After using words you should never use in front of a kid, I observed my stud finder tool buzzing with the little red light going on. Sean was holding it up to my head. Time to stop.

Got out of bed feeling like a wrung out face cloth and laid on the couch immobile with a cup of coffee. I begged Sean to give me 20 minutes.
20 minutes later.
In our driveway, he reached in the car trunk and started sucking on the end of my plastic oil funnel. I took away the guitar tuner, eggbeater, can opener, jar of peanuts, salt shaker, screwdriver, and a left-behind Christmas ornament. Never leave a toddler alone in a room with sparkle glue.

I brought Sean by work today. A guy with a long gray beard was pushing a cart of boxes. Sean said, "Why is Santa pushing boxes?" What could I tell him?
I said, "It's tough all over Sean; Santa has to work two jobs."

Kids hate going to bed. If they only knew that the day will come when they can hardly wait to go to bed.

Our Baby Was Born Premature

Sean started his day laughing because I held up a bowl of Rice Crispies to his ear.

We went to a muffler shop to get the resonator replaced on our car. The guy working under the car had a tattoo of a wrench on his neck and a purple Mohawk haircut. Sean asked me if he was a dinosaur. I made up some kind of -*saurus*.

Sometimes parents agree with children to make the questions go away without listening to what the child is asking.
You are doing something like trying to strap them into their car seat while you're thinking about your back and knee going out, or you're just daydreaming and they're asking away, and you say to them, "Yes, that's right. Yeah. M-hm."
The kid could be saying, "Aunt Betty sure has a nice pear-shaped ass, eh Daddy?"
"Yes, that's right. Yeah. M hm."

Kids know when you aren't listening to them and they will get you back when they're old enough to get a driver's license.

At a department store to buy pants. After unleashing him from his stroller, he ran though all the circular clothing displays with complete abandon, at one point diving on to the floor under a rack of pants only to be dragged out. He kicked while being carried out of the store like a sack of potatoes as I felt my shirt climbing up my back. And he's learned that trick all toddlers learn—the one where they go stiff in your arms. It's almost impossible to carry someone who's stiff. It was L.A.—hot (enough to heat up a slice of pizza) in the parking lot. Why spend the money for a sauna? You can get the same effect during summer by locking yourself in your car in a Los Angeles parking lot.

(the same way he was conceived)

We finally buckled him into his car seat. He asked for water. There was a sippy cup of water lying in the back seat. I gave it to him and said, "This thing has probably been back here for a week."
Maggie through slit eyes, "That'll put him to sleep."

This morning, Sean made sure our cat had enough milk in its bowl. He also made sure the kitchen floor had enough milk.

In the evening, Sean put the plug in the bathroom sink, turned the faucets on, and left the room. He was wearing a fire hat and a baseball cap on top of his fire hat.

They gave all the kids juice boxes on their first day of school. That's like gun powder and a match.

Toddlers at a soccer class move like a busted bag of marbles on a hard wood floor.
I heard the Coach say more than once, "Don't lick the ball." Then there was the kid who stuffed a ball under his shirt and rolled back and forth on the grass.

I ventured into our garage to help throw out old baby clothes with Maggie. Trying to keep a mother from throwing out old baby clothes is like taking a pile of half-empty chili cans from a bear. She held up a one-piece reindeer outfit that had gone hard from stale milk. It felt like a stuffed animal feels after twenty years in a box: crunchy. There was a brown stain all over the reindeer. She held it up for a long time.
We ended up with four-and-a-half boxes out of five still on the shelf. She only threw out half a box. And then with tears in her eyes. She said, "This means we're not having another baby."
   "No, it means we have to throw out four-and-a-half more boxes. Okay, I'm leaving the garage now."

Our Baby Was Born Premature

You know the romance has gone out of your marriage when you're family is sitting in a restaurant waiting for dinner to arrive and you casually lean over and smell your kid's butt to make sure everything's okay—and then you bring your head back up and, as if it's perfectly normal, announce: "Hey, we could bring our friends here."

There are decapitated action figures all over Sean's room. I picked up two sets of legs and couldn't figure out if it was Superman or Spiderman. It's hard to tell a super hero by their under pants.

Today I reached in my jean jacket pocket and pulled out a helicopter. Later, at a café—a siren went off in my backpack.

(the same way he was conceived)

36 MONTHS

At the park, my kid spent his basketball class on the tire swing, the slide, and the ladder—on the other side of the park.

What's worse, sliding on cat yak or twisting an ankle on Thomas the Train?

He came into the living room looking like the cat that swallowed the bird, with his hands behind his back.
"Guess what I have?" he said. I looked.
It was a knife, serrated.
I moved cautiously—and removed it from his hands, once again confirming that a dad's real job is to spend all day preventing his children from dying.

Today an empty jar of peanut butter was in Sean's crib. A tinker toy was in the fridge and a bag of rice was all over the living room floor.

I came home from work tonight and the back door flew open and Sean bolted out on to the driveway wearing a white silk cape. Then he sat on my lap and stared at the stars and the quarter moon with me. I went inside and placed a piece of chicken Maggie had made on a plate. It looked pretty good. It was cooked with sweet and sour sauce. I took the salt-shaker off the counter and added some to my chicken—about half a cup full. Sean had completely loosened the top to the saltshaker and it's nowhere near April Fools.

He took a bag of pretzels into his bedroom, naked. He can have the pretzels.

At the end of the day Mommy said, "Sean's three and I am now three."

Our Baby Was Born Premature

I've seen a lot of parents have Disneyland flashbacks. Their faces turn gaunt and their voices come out as something like a sigh, "You won't get out of there for less than a thousand bucks."
At those prices you'd be better off starting up your old cocaine habit.

While running back and forth.
  "Sean, what's that on your face?"
  "Just dirt, Mommy."

A proud friend of ours was describing how much her three-year-old kid was into music.
"There's not a day goes by that he doesn't play his guitar. And he loves his music class."
I asked her husband about their son's new musical inspiration. He whispered to me, "Sticks, kazoos, and shaker eggs."

Maggie spent her time in the Post office today trying to prevent Sean from running out of the Post office. She accomplished this but ended up with stamps on her forehead. She tried to listen to the clerk while Sean pulled the trigger on his very loud plastic jigsaw he was carrying. It all ended with her having to pay first class instead of book rate.

In a restaurant, Sean is using some crayons on his place mat. I told him, "You have a fine sense of color, Sean."
At which point he snapped his crayon right in half and threw it on the floor.

Is there a worse power than a three-year-old armed with a garden hose?

(the same way he was conceived)   117

YEAR 4

"The stereotypical view of Punch casts him as a deformed, child-murdering, wife-beating psychopath who commits appalling acts of violence and cruelty upon all those around him and escapes scott-free—and is thus greatly enjoyed by small children."

From Wikipedia on the puppet play, Punch and Judy

37 MONTHS

Tomatoes are known as Good Naytoes.

At West Hollywood park, Sean's friend Willow appeared from behind a tree with lipstick on. She told everybody, "It was on the ground for me." Willow's mother said, "Great—my daughter put on lipstick a tranny used the night before."

Play date at Willow's house: She has six pet hamsters. Sean got to hold one. Turns out he wasn't used to something that wiggles . . .
For a long time today, Willow had five hamsters. The poor thing was found hiding under a sofa while a toddler and a preschool kid were stomping around and yelling, "Hamster!"
Finally it showed itself to Willow's mom. It must have recognized adult shoes and ran to them.

I gave Sean some paints, paper, and a stamp set at the kitchen table one foggy morning as I attempted to wake up. One of the stamps was a gorilla. Soon there were three or four gorillas on a piece of paper.
As she passed the table, Maggie looked at the paper and said to Sean, "Look, it's Daddy—ooga booga."

We gave Sean his first pair of shoes that have blinking lights on the bottom. He was running and trying to look at his shoes at the same time by lifting his legs up—which didn't work out too well. I saw a kid at the airport who had wheels on his shoes. On top of everything else, parents are now worried that their kid might roll away from home.

Saw a minivan with a bumper sticker. It said, "My kid was student of the month."
You never see a bumper sticker that says, "My kid writes a "d" like a "b.""

Sean has had a new stuffed toy, lamby, for about one week. It now has a name.
"Eyeless the Lamby."

Not even bribery could stop Sean from taking his clothes off at the park today.
"I hot Daddy."
Off they came.
I was once the prodigal son, setting off to conquer the world. Now I'm retrieving pants in a park while holding Goldfish crackers.

My day off. The coffee I had set on automatic brew the night before was now a coffee ground lake on the floor that ran down the counter. The empty pot was sitting on the counter instead of in the coffee machine, resulting in coffee mud everywhere. After setting the coffee lab back up, I shuffled into the living room and saw a beetle sitting on the wall like it was thinking, "Just stay still and maybe he won't see me ... "
I caught it in a glass before Maggie saw it and went into convulsions. She has been known to find insects in the house and text me a link to a web site of the species.
"It has mandibles! Pincers for seizing and biting food!"
I decided to release it behind the garage, and in return I asked the beetle to "please tell all the other bugs to stay out of our house."
Sean woke up.
He has pink eye.

38 MONTHS

The flu. Day 4. Maggie called to tell me Sean wasn't taking his medicine. I told her to throw his devices out onto the street or lock him in his room and force the medicine on him. He cried so much he was sick to his stomach. So much for my career as a child therapist. After a visit to Urgent Care, the doctor on call recommended suppositories in case Sean started throwing up a lot. Now—if I was vomiting and someone stuck something up my ass at the exact same time—I'm almost positive I'd keep vomiting.

Sean was overjoyed on a neighbor's trampoline. I sat there nursing a beer thinking, "What if the kid lands in the space with the rusty springs and the steel circular tube and then there's a twisted ankle and blood, broken bones, screaming, massive hospital bills and he will be sidelined from school, which means he'll fall behind and not get into college."

Today he made a water cake. One of our Pyrex dishes filled with water. Then you add a six inch toy fighter plane. Ready to serve.

"What are is those?

"

If I don't eat a proper breakfast before engaging my kid, I will experience a low-blood-sugar nervous breakdown around mid-morning. After coffee, I fried some bacon and eggs and made toast and included a seasoned pork chop on my plate, which was left over from dinner the night before.
Things Sean did at the table:
Stood on his chair. Was told to sit. Sat. Stood on his chair, again. Opened the refrigerator. Wanted whipped cream squirted into his hand. Took the bacon off my plate. Shoved his hand down his pants. Grabbed something in there.

(the same way he was conceived)

I had one bite of my egg sandwich.

Sean spit up all over the kitchen table. Milk, egg, bread, and bacon bits. Some of which pooled on his plate.

I got up and used some paper towels to clean off the table while Sean was punching my arm saying, "I sick Daddy!" I wasn't finished cleaning up when I decided to stop and take my second bite of egg sandwich.

Mommy entered the kitchen and what she saw was a father eating an egg sandwich not paying attention to a puke covered table and baby arm.

After her reaction—I thought about what people must experience when they have a stroke.

We cleaned Sean up at the sink.

I reheated my egg sandwich in the microwave, got back to the table, and noticed my pork chop was MIA. I actually looked through the trash, thinking Maggie may have thrown it out in frustration. It was not in there.

I sat back down to eat my Sunday breakfast. I looked under the table.

The cat had finished half my pork chop and was tearing the rest of it like only a cat can.

39 MONTHS

We have a small house and my shoes are gone. Maggie is on the phone with a friend, watching me banging drawers and crouching down to peer under beds and chairs, and she laughs, "He's going nuts, and he's wearing white shorts and brown socks!"
The shoes were under old clothes in the laundry hamper.
Sean explains this as "I put them in a safe place."
And then he won't tell me where the safe place is. Now, I have lost the book I was just reading.

It started with the bedcover. Maggie had it balled up and she shoved it into my face.
"Smell this. I just washed it—but does it smell like piss?"
I said, "I don't think so." And she took it away.
Later she pushed something else in my face, a towel I think, and said, "Tell me if you think this smells like piss?"
And then she said, "No—well, how about in the middle then?"
I kept saying no.
I got her back by using furniture polish on our hardwood floor.
Maggie came in the room like someone who had never been on a curling rink before.

When Sean takes eggs out of the fridge he makes sure they're fresh by shaking the box.

(the same way he was conceived)   123

40 MONTHS

Father's Day. Three time-outs. It's only noon. He broke his fever and then broke some of his toys.

I asked our neighbor what my son's name was.
He said, "Sean."
I told him, "Really, because he doesn't respond at all when I call him that."

He came out of the bathroom muttering something about a poo tooth brush. This was echoed by very concerned parents.
It turned out he was talking about Winnie.

Sean actually wanted to take a bath. The reason: I bought some miniature plastic frogmen action figures and a submarine.

Is there anything scarier than teaching a child to sew? Even with a Mother's expert guidance, the result was a zig-zag border going through a cotton leg of the cat with the fiddle. The running frying pan didn't make it either. And the laughing cow jumping over the moon had sewn balls of thread all over its body.
Oh well, little baby shirts and onesies are going in the mail to her nephew anyway. From the crazy aunt.

Our Baby Was Born Premature

41 MONTHS

"We don't put jelly beans in our nose." That's something I never thought I'd say in my life.

Sean made Daddy a treat for breakfast. It was sitting next to his plate of uneaten toast on the kitchen table. A saucepan of Corn Puffs cereal mixed with orange juice. Basically vomit.

I cleaned out my Coleman cooler and put it in the sun to dry. About an hour later, an inch of sand filled the bottom of it. Close by, on the ground, lay a yellow cement truck and a plastic blue shovel.

He did a number-two in the toilet all by himself today and told the gardener. I had to bring him home a reward. He requested a helicopter. I found a matchbox red helicopter. You press a button and lights come on and a loud speaker on the front of it works. "Suspects spotted! Lower the spotlight!" After several hours of this, I threatened to take the helicopter into the yard and bury it.

No matter how short the distance—three-year-olds always run to get there.

Today I held onto his hands and spun him in a circle until we were really dizzy; and then he asked for a pair of scissors.

My parents are in their 80s. They said they can hardly wait to take care of Sean and give me a break. What this really means is my vacation in northern Ontario will be spent watching them watching Sean.

(the same way he was conceived)

At the airport Sean found moving floors far more interesting than non-moving floors. I went up and down the entire departure area 17 times.

On a tip from a friend, I brought some bubble gum on the plane—kind of like a first aid kit in case of emergency. I had to administer a stick about an hour into the flight.

Why do toddlers finally fall asleep when the captain announces the plane is about to land?"

Grandpa: "There's a bug in your cup."
Sean: "Where'd that come from?"
Grandpa: "It jumped in there."
Sean: "Where'd it jump in from?"
Grandpa: "It flew around in the sky."
Sean: "Where'd the sky come from?"

Sean not listening to his dad at the shore.
"Hey Sean look at the duck."
Sean's thinking, *Yeah whatever, I've got a pail of mud.*
A little bit later he told me he was—"building a hole."

After changing his diaper, it seemed impossible and yet there it was—a blue marble in his bum. What are the odds of sitting him directly on top of a marble!?
I should take him to Vegas.

Our Baby Was Born Premature

Going to a small town in Canada is better than Disneyland for a parent. Some lawns have tractors on them and it doesn't cost $500 to see them. We saw a crane lifting a cement ring above some trees, a steam shovel digging a pit, and a backhoe on a barge. Not even Mickey Mouse can compete with a back hoe on a barge.

A cousin of mine gave Sean a purple, soft-rubber dragon. I asked Sean what the dragon's name was and he said, "Grandma."

Took Sean out on a lake. It was a beautiful day. The cottages along the piney shore, the waves rollicking and spraying all around our boat, the wind, the trees.
All Sean wanted to do was press the red button which sounded the horn.

My parent's fridge is a picture shrine to their Grandson. They need to throw some different pics up there—even a cat would help. I'm lucky; they keep them up out of love not because they can't remember who he is.

Every time I go to the airport I want to get into at least two fist fights. Where else do you pay $5 for a bottle of water?
Sean decided to turn my luggage into a shuttle bus. My suitcase has wheels and he straddled the entire case and told me how fast to go. Everyone got a kick out of watching Sean on my bag.
We arrived at the gate. A little boy named Leo was playing with some plastic animals. His father was balding. Sean said Leo had asked him why his hair went to heaven?
We boarded the plane. On the way to our seat Sean yelled at everyone, "I'm going to see my mom!"
He high five'd a few passengers.

(the same way he was conceived)

I decided I would test my bravery as a dad. My mission? To be present every moment with my child for the entire flight and not pussy out with electronic devices like most dads. I will never quit. I thrive on adversity. I am physically harder. I am mentally stronger than my enemies. My back-pack was armed with unopened toys. Sean did not know this. I prayed these toys would buy me five hours—the length of time it takes to get back to LA.

1st toy

A tin of plastic army soldiers. We kick ass. So much so that I have to tell Sean to stop kicking the seat in front of him. It would be quite a scene if the guy in front swallowed his peach with the pit still in it. An hour passed. Soldiers are good toys.

2nd toy

After failing miserably to draw a plane and a spaceship for Sean I told him I have a "suitcase of stamps."
It was a suitcase the size of a box of raisins with six stamps and a red ink tray inside it. Stamps of a boat, a train, and some trucks. He was busy stamping his notebook. He seemed to enjoy pressing hard enough to make the ink pad look like it was bleeding. He was really into the fire truck stamp. The ink was everywhere. He looked like he got lost in a raspberry patch. I took a bite of the complimentary cheese snack and it tasted like ink. He was stamping fire trucks all over his book.

3rd toy

Thomas the Train sticker pack. He tore into them. Parents of toddlers use the word "WOW" in a fake-natural-expression-of-amazement kind of way in order to keep the child from losing interest in something. Judging from the placement of the stickers, he created the worst Thomas Train wreck in history.

4th toy

A couple of hours into the flight, and I realized that my bag of what I thought was foam sticker animals have no stickers on them. This toy was useless.

Our Baby Was Born Premature

5th toy
You must always have reserve stickers. I pulled out a book of funny stickers for blank faces. You get to make up your own face with the stickers. Sean did his best to copy the great Dada artists of the past. This worked long enough for me to notice I would not be drinking from the same bottle of water I gave Sean. It looked like a fish aquarium when you first sprinkle the food into it from his crackers and pretzels. Then he had to pee. Taking a toddler into an airplane lavatory is like trying to assemble a kite in a phone booth. And then fly it.

6th toy
Tube of plastic dinosaurs. Worked for about 20 minutes.
The captain announced we were heading into turbulence and to fasten seat belts. Sean looked at me and said, "I have to poo pee." Not sure what class I was sitting in on the airplane, but every time I had to get out of my seat it was like giving the senior lady next to me a lap dance. I half expected her to tip me a twenty.

7th toy
A plastic robot filled with water. You push the buttons and it shoots little rings around inside the water. The object of the game is to settle the rings on tiny spears. I adjusted the golf-ball-size aircraft light above me to spotlight the robot. This was a pretty good time killer. He pulled a Houdini. The seat belt could no longer hold him.

8th toy
A box of raisins. He poured them out on his tray. I noticed the woman behind me with a boy a little younger than Sean. She also had a daughter—maybe a year older. They were both in her arms, quietly listening to her read a story.
Sean was trying to show me how he was using the tiny robot pincer-hands to pick up raisins in order to serve himself. I'm keeping up with the mom behind me in my own way.

(the same way he was conceived)

9th toy
A story book about Bugs Bunny going to a party thrown by Porky Pig and Daffy Duck. Five minutes.

10th toy
Rubber, stretchy animals. He played with them for a few minutes and then gathered 5 pounds of toys and tried stuffing them into a 1 pound bag.

11th toy
I pulled out the in-case-of-emergency toy. A chocolate bar in the shape of a ghost.

We landed. I made it. My backpack of toys worked, and I didn't even have to pull out the paint set or the purple putty. I got all the toys at the dollar store, which everyone knows has everything you need—except self esteem. It all cost only $13.

LAX. The palm trees, cab drivers fighting over tourists luggage. Home sweet home. Mommy picks us up at the airport. Soon we're driving through a tunnel with the windows down. Sean is yabbering in the backseat about a robot while I'm trying to tell his mom all about our trip—she yells over us, "I can't hear anything!"

Our Baby Was Born Premature

42 MONTHS

Still no pants on and its noon.

Bob and Joan showed up with their two boys, Jacob and Danny—four and two-and-a-half years. We ventured to the nearby park. Danny, the younger one, was intent on trying to figure out how the water fountain worked.
I said to Bob as we sat like a couple of retired World War II veterans on a park bench, "Danny is delighted, focusing on that water fountain."
Bob said, "Danny is delighted, focusing on anything Jacob doesn't try to take away from him."

We went to the beach and Sean ran around in a circle holding a sandwich, which soon became—just that ... then he handed it to his mother.

Washing a car with a three-year-old.
"Put the soap bubbles on the car not on my pants, please."
"Be careful of the door, it's very heavy and stay inside the car—Daddy is going to spray the car, okay?"
"SHUT THE DOOR!"
"Don't lick the hood, it's dirty."
"Get out of the trunk."
"Put the road flare back, please."
"Give me the gum. It's old."
"No, not the change tray. Close it."
"Turn the vacuum back on, please."
Five seconds later. "Sean, turn it on!"
"Thank you."
Ten seconds later. "To the highest setting, please."
"Leave the vacuum alone."
"Out of the car with your bowl of raspberries."

(the same way he was conceived)

43 MONTHS

Ga sheen = machine.

Tonight Sean wanted a mushroom cheese pizza—hold the mushrooms, hold the tomato sauce, hold the dough.

Little kids are all color blind. They don't care about gender, either. All they want to do is play.

I asked Sean's friend Nick, who's three-and-a-half, what his nickname was and then realized his name was Nick. No wonder he didn't answer me.

44 MONTHS

Pretty sure only a three-and-a-half-year-old stands in the check-out line at a Drug Store holding a tooth brush in one hand and a package of Pez in the other.

Sean's been helping around the kitchen in different ways, such as counting spoonfuls of coffee beans. He took a scoop and poured it into the grinder and counted, "one," and then did it again, "two." He got to three, but he poured two scoops; and then got to four and poured more scoops in the grinder and said, "five." By now there were nine or ten scoops in the grinder. It was time to grind the beans which he did without the top secured to the grinder. And we all know what happens when you do that.

Sean started his day by putting on one green sock and one blue sock. That's okay—there is a girl in his preschool we call, "the one-shoe-on-one-shoe-off girl."

I decided to get him in the car and go to the Big Lots department store.
In my shopping cart: two robots, one real-sound chainsaw, one super transport truck, one helicopter, one Hulk on a tank, one rescue snowmobile, one talking cow head on a stick.
All I came in here for was a paint brush.

Sean has been watering the stump in the front yard—for 10 minutes.

I went to a pumpkin patch today with Sean's preschool class and a bunch of nervous moms (some towing two children), moms who are pleasant on the surface but are one less sip of coffee away from murder.

(the same way he was conceived)   133

There was hay, goats, and lots of pumpkins. There were lots of other preschool classes there, too. I personally ruined about 11 class photos.

It was nice to take the morning off work and spend some quality time with Sean. That is, until he had a sobbing tantrum because he wasn't dressed as a Power Ranger, like another boy.

Day 30 of my all-plant-based diet. My pee is the same color as a barber shop pole. That's good, right?

Maggie: "We're eating whole wheat?"
Me: "Meat?"
Maggie: "I'm going to make a salad with beets."
Me: "Meat?"
Maggie: "Wash the spinach leaves."
Me: "Meat?"

It all started because I got sucked in by one of those vegetarian documentaries. The guy could pitch me an all beer diet and I'd buy it. Some buff Ausie guy,

"Right mate, welcome to Oscar's all beer diet. I fell down the stairs four times today, and I feel bloody great!"

I've decided not to be too hard on myself about letting my kid eat a hot dog every now and then. I've also decided to make friends with vegans because if the zombie apocalypse comes I will kill and eat vegans—for the nutrients.

"I am need that" and "I like my tacos real much."

Gluten free, wheat free, sugar free, salt free, lactose free, dairy free, cruelty free. And then they charge you a fortune.

◈

Our Baby Was Born Premature

45 MONTHS

I took a different route to the preschool. There are a lot of stop signs on our street, like maybe 30. And Sean laughed at me all the way and yelled at every stop sign, "You're a bad, Daddy!" Apparently, I never came to a complete stop.

Sean's most popular question lately: "How why?"

"Daddy, I have an idea! How 'bout I watch TV and have breakfast in the living room?"
We just walked away.

I stopped him and said, "Never ever try picking up a cat by the ears while in your underwear."

(the same way he was conceived)

46 MONTHS

Maggie was given two boxes of Sees chocolates. We decided to give one to our mailman. This was explained to me the morning Maggie left to do some errands.

The mailman showed up and I handed Sean the bigger of the two boxes of chocolates. The postman was at the next door neighbor's house and Sean ran down the sidewalk holding the big red box of chocolates.

Mommy walked into the kitchen an hour or so later.

"Where's my chocolates?"

I told her Sean gave them to the mailman.

The only word that can describe the reaction.

Fire.

She went on to tell me she had placed the smaller box of choco-lates in the mailbox. This previous conversation, I had absolutely no memory of, which made things *far* worse.

Christmas Eve and we're not talking to each other.

Eventually Maggie unlocked the bedroom door and said a few words to me, "You don't care" among them.

Christmas morning, halfway through opening presents; someone had given us a family present which consisted of a large chocolate "P" for me, a large chocolate "S" for Sean and a large chocolate "M" for Maggie.

I started eating the M until Maggie spotted me from across the room.

"What the Hell are you doing!"

Trying to take chocolate away from a postpartum mom twice in 24 hours. That takes balls.

Sean and Nick are jumping around in the house.
Nick yells, "Let's play hide and seek!"
Sean: "Okay!"
Nick yells again, "I'll hide!"
Sean points at Nick and yells back, "And you seek!"
"Yaaah,"
They both run in separate directions.

(the same way he was conceived)

47 MONTHS

New game.
Upside Down 'Til The Honey Comes Out.
Maggie lifts Sean upside down and squeezes him.

There are whole bookshelves at Barnes & Noble or Chapters covering what can go wrong with your baby. Wayward Girl. Clepto at Five. What To Do If Your 2 Year Old Enjoys Wine. Dad is a 3 letter word so is Ass. There are no good-news parenting books.

I came home to find Sean and his little friend Nicholas playing in the house. I think they were throwing things at each other, and then I heard a thud and then rumbling?
Sean's mom walked by and casually said to the children—but also more in general, "Go right ahead and smother yourself. It's a quiet activity."

"Ice cream is good for your body and your teeth, Daddy."
Nice try.

I popped a cracker into my mouth. It seemed damp. It smelled, too.
Maggie, watching me, said, "Um, Sean licked all the tuna off his tuna cracker sandwiches today."
Christ—I almost puked.

After a long day Maggie is in the arm chair leaning forward with her head in her hands. Sean has a specific way of wearing his PJ bottoms, which he is now demonstrating. He somehow stuffs both his legs into one pant leg and then attempts to shuffle around the room and says,
"Look Mommy, I'm a penguin!"
Mommy didn't lift up her head to look.

(the same way he was conceived)

We watched from the kitchen table, refusing to leave our coffees as Sean used his "midget helper" (which is his stool), to get a cup from the cupboard.

Then he opened the fridge and tried to balance a jug of milk on the edge of the refrigerator door (no hands.) And yet, we were immobile. He finally stopped the torment after I used a swear word which Maggie corrected immediately.

According to Mommy, "stupid" is the worst thing you can say to a child. Sean never fails to correct me now, "Daddy, stupid's not a nice word. You owe me a quarter."

I agreed to go to Chuck E. Cheese's like a cat agrees to go to the vet while in a pillowcase. Maggie said, "It's for one of Sean's little friends. C'mon."

Chuck E. Cheese's was like hundreds of kids climbing in a plastic Habitrail. None of them had shoes on and half of them had runny noses. The carpet throughout the restaurant smelled like ground-in French fries on the floor of a city bus. Games that dispensed nothing but tickets you couldn't seem to redeem anywhere were the reason kids kept pounding buttons on vending machines all over the restaurant. They didn't care what the buttons do; they just wanted to pound them. Parents and children feverishly carried around stacks of tickets in their pockets for no reason. At one of these games, (a miniature bowling alley game) the alley next to us was spewing out a roll of tickets as Sean tossed balls everywhere but where he was supposed to. I told him, "Get your tickets!" Then I realized they weren't ours because Sean was obviously not winning anything.

The look on the face of the father next to me said "Do you want to take this outside?"

Sean never paid attention to me because he was too busy running toward another game which had squirt guns.

A Chuck E. Cheese employee, who probably lost the coin toss, came out dressed as Chuck E. Cheese: a huge rat. He waved to about 40 birthday parties going on at the same time in a small room. A video projection of singers blasted out a dance tune and cakes and balloons and pizza and soda with lots of sugar were everywhere. That's the smell of Parmesan and vomit, folks.

It's the end of America.

Sean cried because he didn't want to leave. Until someone gave him a bag of candy.

Reprise to Chuck E. Cheese's story:

A neighbor told me his Chuck E. Cheese's story. He went to his nephew's party, and in the midst of all the Chuck E. Cheese noise, he was cornered by one of his sister-in-law's friends, who tried to explain eternal damnation for people who are without faith in the Lord.

He said it was the closest he ever came to ripping another human beings eyeballs out. And that his wife still owes him for that day—two years ago.

I have never been hit in the balls this much in my life. Fathers who have two kids must be on the ground all the time.

It didn't happen this much when I played hockey. Maybe I should wear a cup again?

The night before Sean's birthday was so insane that I must retell it with only slight embellishments. Sean is running a fever. Maggie takes his temperature. 100.

Maggie says, "You have to take some medicine, Sean."

Sean says, "I think I have a beaver."

We give him Strawberry chewable Tylenol. He coughs and after a drink of water says, "I think I know why I am sick."

   "Why is that, Sean?"

   "Because I picked my nose."

1:00 a.m. The over-protective parents' ear thermometer says 101.

(the same way he was conceived)

The crying child with children's pink Tylenol liquid all over his shirt that he refused to swallow is fireman-carried by Daddy into the car behind the house. He's half dressed. And I mean Daddy.

Mommy has all the windows down and the air-conditioning is blasting. She steps on it.

Racing up Torrance Blvd. At the intersection of something and something there are police cars everywhere. What a terrible time for a sting operation. The light is red and Daddy howls, "Blow through it!"

Mommy yells, "I NEED AN ESCORT!"

Daddy screams out the window, "MY SON HAS A COMMON HEAD COLD GET OUT OF THE WAY!"

The plastic syringe full of kid's Tylenol is rolling back and forth on the dash board.

A police car squeals after Mommy and Daddy but Mommy and Daddy lose him within a few blocks of the hospital as the cop car spins out of control and destroys a mail box. We screech into the emergency at Little Company of Mary hospital.

Daddy holds his kid while trotting across the driveway, "My son has a temperature of 99!"

The pediatrician informs the over-protective parents that ear thermometers are not accurate and that the story of a high temperature giving a child brain damage is nothing but a wives' tale.

Daddy says to the Doctor, "Ya, kids high temperatures give parents brain damage."

As for the party the next day—a lot of kids showed up, and I got a lot of pictures of kids eating cupcakes, which basically looks like a bear in a trash can of honey.

I guess a four-year-old's birthday party is a success when the guests leave crying.

YEAR 5

"If you want your children to turn out well,
spend twice as much time with them and half
as much money."

- Abigail Van Buren

49 MONTHS

He's getting so smart. I miss him as an imbecile. And let's face it—
up to four years of age, kids are imbeciles. They'll walk out in front
of a bus. They can't even put their own pants on.

Went to Adventure City—the poor man's Disneyland. Sean likes
three out of fifteen rides. The train, the firetruck, and the petting
Zoo (which isn't actually a ride, although some kids think it is.)
Nothing scares a Rooster more than a kid.
At the petting zoo, you can feed the goats and chickens with the
cone part of an ice cream cone which they fill with pellets and seed
for a buck. One small child held out his cone and a goat licked it
and the kid decided to eat it. The kid's mom was a second too late,
"Noooo!"
Amazingly the kid did it again—and Mommy was too late—again.
That's like Herpes Simplex Type 500 isn't it?
All the parents by the fence watching laughed and laughed.
Saw another little boy lying on the ground wailing.
After we took in some more of Sean's "same rides" it was time for
lunch. I saw the same little kid who was on the ground earlier—still
wailing—this time in a line.
Popcorn never tastes as good as it smells at an amusement park.
Sean has been asking to go to the potty a lot in public. He has
gone three times and it's only noon. And what is scarier than a
public toilet at a carnival where the key is attached to an old con-
taminated piece of 2x4. Thanks for the thrills Adventure City.

Sean started his day by seeing what happens to an egg if you drop
it on a tile floor from a height of four feet.

His poo is green. Whatever.

50 MONTHS

Sean found a box of condoms in a bedroom drawer. I told him they were party balloons.

Sean's first lemonade stand is apple juice but it will do. A woman walked by the house and Sean ran over to her. Handing her a cup of juice, he said, "A quarter please."
We had to explain that the customer has to *ask* for the juice—you can't just force them to buy something.
We told her: "It's okay, you can have it."
She drank it and gave the rest to one of her kids and then walked away without giving Sean a quarter. If you can't spare a quarter for a kid, you should stop having kids.

Maggie called me at work. She was simmering.
"Everyone in Sean's class was invited to Chantel's birthday party except Sean."
The clouds kept rolling in—rumbling low.
I said, "Aren't we going to two four-year-old's birthday parties this weekend?"
Maggie: "Yes—but every kid in the class, Paul."
I tried to fathom what was going on.
"So ... we don't have to go to a third birthday party? Maggie, that's the best news I've heard all day."
She hung up the phone.

We drove halfway across the city to attend another birthday party. It was at Griffith Park by an old train station—a place called, Travel Town. There must have been 50 kids there. L.A. parents set the toddler birthday party bar at 50 guests. You have to drop at least five grand or move out-of-state, where the toddler b-day parties are more affordable.
Skippy the Train Clown showed up and gathered the four-year-olds and started going hoarse attempting to keep them engaged with

(the same way he was conceived) 145

games and magic tricks. All the kids were in a semi-circle in front of Skippy and he was performing a magic trick.

"Hey kids, watch what happens when I drop this stone into my magic happy bag."

My kid stood up in front of Skippy, bent over with his butt in Skippy's direction and said, "I'm a stinky skunk."

As one who appreciates theater and live comedy performance, I thought this was nothing short of spectacular.

Skippy just said, "Yeah, whatever kid," and continued his act. Skippy probably went home, set his happy bag down, put a .38 barrel in his mouth. And ka-boom.

At Starbucks, I handed a twenty to the girl at the cashier for a grande coffee. She gave me my cup of coffee and my 17 odd dollars in change and pushed my twenty back at me across the counter and then went on with her work. I stood there momentarily thinking about my getaway, and then decided to push my twenty dollar bill back across the counter and said, "Excuse me I think this is yours."

I winked.

She thanked me.

That evening I went to Longs Drugs to buy a pack of Pullups. I found a Sponge Bob toothbrush for $2 and threw that in there as well. The woman at the cash register ran my card. Four bucks! I stared at the receipt. Instead of running the expensive pack of Pullups and the tooth brush, she ran the tooth brush twice.

Later I told Maggie and Sean about the phenomenon.

"My superpower is making people give me incorrect change in my favor," I said. "I'm Discount Man!"

My kid got off his mom's lap and said, "Daddy, that's the stupidest superpower I've ever heard."

Our Baby Was Born Premature

51 MONTHS

"Read the story from the googending."

Being four-and-a-half has its advantages. There aren't many other times in your life you can stand on a toilet seat while you brush your teeth.

It was Dad's Day at preschool. Fathers were supposed to do two hours with their kids. As I left the house, I told Maggie, "We're gonna eat steaks at preschool today."
I showed up with Sean. Some dads momentarily lost control of their boys who cried while lying on the ground, and I kept it to myself when Sean stroked another father's back with a green marker without the guy knowing it.
We all assembled crazy shit no one will keep, and Dad's Day at preschool came to a close. Sean and I left. We held hands and unlatched the gate that leads out of the play area, and I looked over my shoulder as we walked across the parking lot. I saw Blake (one of Sean's buddies) using all his splayed appendages like Spider Man to prevent his father from getting him into the back seat of their car.

I'm not going to spank a four-year-old. It's not a fair fight. You can't have two extremely different weight classes going at it like that. They won't even do that in Vegas. The only time in life you should be spanked is if you enjoy it.

There's this kid in Sean's preschool. Anders. He always shows up in track pants, a turtleneck, and a fleece vest. If his parents don't get it together—Anders is going to be in serious trouble with the ladies.

(the same way he was conceived)   147

"One more full up."
Sean has turned me into a waitress at Denny's—you know the gal who constantly refills your coffee cup, sometimes as you are taking it to your lips.

"The baby kangaroo rides in the Mommy kangaroo's couch."

Our Baby Was Born Premature

52 MONTHS

Drove halfway across L.A. to an Imax theater so Sean could experience *Prehistoric Sea Creatures* in 3-D. Paid $35 and then paid for popcorn and sat down. The opening scene had a pterodactyl fly right at the audience—his beak about three feet from us. Sean cried, dropped his popcorn, and I carried him out of the theater. Daddy maxed out at the Imax.

Last day of preschool all the moms and kids went to a nearby park for a picnic. Jaquine's brother ate four water bugs.
A little kid was balling his eyes out. Sean went over to him and offered him his bike. This is a huge leap for a human being because it shows he has empathy and that's what separates us from the hominids. The school he's going to has helped—we think.
I'm still going to enroll him in Karate and kick boxing as soon as possible, though.

"Eat your asparagus, Sean."
"But I want sauce on it, Daddy."
"What kind of sauce do you put on asparagus, Sean?"
"Chocolate sauce."
Another no nutrition meal. The third this week.

53 MONTHS

Young woman: "Are you going to preschool or kindergarten?"
Sean: "I'm going to a spaceship in the park."

Mommy's new name is Butt Mommy. When Mommy tells him its bed time. "But Mommy!"

Took him to the museum. It is undergoing a multi-million dollar rebuild on one side of the landmark building. Out of the historical brick and mortar now sits six stories of multi-colored metal origami shards jutting into the sky.
How do you get funding to make art travesties?
"They may as well have had a half million dollar endowment for a big ass coming out of the museum walls."
I hadn't been to the Museum of History in a long time and it was nice to see they've continued the tradition of closing the famous dinosaur exhibit "due to construction."
What's the point in going to a museum with a four-year-old if the dinosaur exhibit is closed?
"How much to get in?"
 Fifteen bucks.
"Okay. What exhibits are open?"
 The water fountain circa 2005 by the lavatories.
"Thanks."

Electric = Goalectric

Our new neighbors go to church on Sunday. They have a three-year-old girl named Eve. I told Maggie, "We'll break them soon."
Eve was in her summer knit dress and Sean asked her to play. She said, "But its Sunday."
Sean said, "Why is there a Sunday?"
Eve didn't answer—she just twirled around and waited for her parents. Her father finally came out to the car wearing a short sleeve, white, starched shirt and tie. To me, that would be like wearing a plaster cast around my neck. This is the same guy who hoards Lego in his garage. Sean jams with him—their version of a garage band.
Sean said to Eve, "Okay—when you get back maybe we can blow bubbles."

Belt grow = Velcro

GAME:
Lying in bed with Sean at night.
"Oh my God! I'm so tired I can hardly wait to lay down on my pillow."
This is his cue to pull the pillow away as I'm slowly reclining. I bounce my head off the mattress.
"HEY! What happened to my pillow!"
He laughs and laughs. And then it's his turn, which (because of his four-year-old voice) is infinitely better for the soul.

(the same way he was conceived)

55 MONTHS

We accompanied Maggie to the doctor's office for a visit the other day. Sean coughed several times. A nurse asked him why he was coughing?
Sean said, "Because I was eating broccoli."

The kid was in the bathroom with his mom. She said, "Sean get out."
Before he left he said, "Don't worry Mommy; one day you'll grow a pee pee."
On his way out he asked why Mommy peed out of her butt?
No amount of schooling prepares you to answer that.

Stride Rights—the most expensive shoes you can buy—being dragged along asphalt feels like the nails-across-the-chalkboard thing.

I turned away for a moment when Sean was in his first public bathroom stall; suddenly he was standing in the middle of the bathroom with his trousers around his ankles.
"I went poop."
Wow—only people in asylums can get away with that.

56 MONTHS

Kids love to believe in things they can't see.
Sean's a minute into a play date with his neighbor Eve. He runs out the door holding an invisible walkie-talkie,
"Snow White, do you read me, over?"
He goes back inside. The next time he came out the door was his last time.
"I don't want to be a supermodel."

"What did you broughted?"
This happens every time I come home with groceries.

Maggie came up with a great way to avoid giving candy to our kid on Halloween. We stick to the rituals, including the gathering of candy at stranger's doors, but then at the end of the evening, before bedtime, we offer him a choice.
"Sean, do you want to keep all your candy or give all your candy away to the Great Pumpkin in exchange for a toy he will bring you in the night?"
He has picked the Great Pumpkin two years in a row. This year he got a plane. The plane didn't work but that's okay—we got to give away all the candy, which is like making the hard choice to flush cocaine down a toilet.

(the same way he was conceived)

57 MONTHS

Mothers come up to me and call me by name, and then I have to go and ask other mothers what the other mothers' names are before the end of the party. Sometimes I'll call a kid the wrong name in front of their parent and find out about it later, and the parent doesn't even correct me. I guess you're safe if you call kids by animals or gourds.
"Hi Pumpkin," or "Hey, nice to see you Squirrel."

I remembered when I took Sean to a Toys R Us to get some play sand. I always thought they should have called that store, "Put it Back," or "You've Already Got One of Those R Us."

Kids never stop filling buckets with sand even when it's blowing in their face.

Crash.
Sean taped a fork, a spoon, and a knife to the side of our refrigerator. After one day—the knife had finally had enough.

Daddy: "Sean, where'd ya get this big blue ball?"
Sean: "At the ball store."
Mom: "The ball store is Eve's house."

Sean threw up a fish stick. Our cat rushed in to investigate under the kitchen table. And he ate it. I wonder if he told our other cat about it.
"Hey, vomited fish on the floor! Do you copy?"
Our other cat running in from lounging on top of our fresh folded laundry in the bedroom, "Copy that. I'm on it!"
All the other cats on our street, "Hey, Dya hear? The cats in that house get to eat puked fish. Ahh, the good life. ABC, baby—already been chewed."

Sean on the tennis court with his friend Elliot.
"Strike 1, strike 2, strike 3 . . . you're out."
Time to enroll him in more sports classes.

Mommy showed Sean his Preemie outfit, which she's kept enshrined in an airless plastic bag kept in a safe that's sealed in a vault.

To begin their day, all the kids in Sean's Pre-K are forced to recite the Pledge of Allegiance, from which the most popular phrase is "Indibizible under God."

They're warning us the kids have to be able to spell their name and sit still for 30 minutes or they'll be held back from kindergarten!? When I went to Kindergarten, my goal was to figure out how to tie my shoe by the end of the year.
There's a rumor that by 3rd grade they want kids to be able to split atoms for the Department of Defense.
They're not horses—they're not supposed to stand a few hours after birth.

Let a four-year-old-boy use an electric pencil sharpener and all the pencils in your house will be one inch long.

When we go to a restaurant, I'm the one that colors on the kid's coloring place mat that the waiter has provided, with crayons. At I-Hop today, I did the bear in green and the wolf in red and stayed inside the lines.
The most popular conversation in restaurants when there is a toddler at the table is "Don't blow your milk—drink your milk."

(the same way he was conceived)

Our kid is about to enter elementary school, so I went to my first educator seminar to listen to a guest educator speak. Apparently, there are eight intelligences, including math, linguistic, spatial, extrovert, interpersonal. The person who doesn't have spatial intelligence is the one who can't fit luggage into an overhead compartment on a plane, until someone who has spatial intelligence helps out by turning the luggage a few degrees—and then everyone can sit. The parents are told to check-mark the intelligence that applies to their kid, and on the last page they can compare their check-marks with famous people who have the same intelligences—according to this speaker. My kid matched Mother Theresa and Ronald Reagan, which means he is going to be the President of the United States while wearing a religious dress.

All I know for sure is that *The Gingerbread Man* is the worst children's bedtime story ever written. It says on the back of the book, "Approved by educators for children 5-8."
Quick synopsis: A little kid opens an oven door while it's on! A gingerbread man jumps out and runs away from every single person he encounters, refusing to stop or listen to anyone. At the end of the story he is cannibalized by a sadistic, serial-killing fox. I quote, "And snip snap—he opened his mouth!"
The End.
Okay lights out—good night, Sean.

How to get Mommy to stop whatever she's doing.
Sean: "It's okay to put orange juice in my water gun, right?"

In my bathtub tonight: two orange rubber snakes and a purple Joker action figure.

Our Baby Was Born Premature

58 MONTHS

Saw a van with 12 sticker kids on the windshield and the sticker-dad was lying down with a bottle of whiskey in his hand.

"DONE GOING POOPEE!"
The whole neighborhood can hear this every time Sean is finished in our bathroom because in southern California your windows are open all year round. This is my cue to go in there and clean him with a wet nap, which he claims he's too small to do, yet.
"DONE GOING POOPEE!"
I wonder if you'd hear that if you stood on the White House lawn?

It's very simple. If I want him to stay inside I say, "Hey Sean, let's go to the park."
If I want him to go outside I say, "Hey Sean, let's stay inside today."

"Daddy, why do they call it a girl cheese sandwich?"

When my kid was three I thought he was hyper active until I saw a kid at the park about the same age standing on a hill, his pants around his ankles, with a toy pistol in each hand pointed at the sky—and he was peeing. I turned to another dad on the bench and I said, "That's the kid you want first so you don't have any more, right?"

In my bathtub is a soggy roll of TP and a wind-up speed boat.

(the same way he was conceived)

59 MONTHS

I've been volunteered to babysit a little girl two doors down because Maggie is going to attend another parent seminar. The neighbors, Russ and Sloan, have two little girls. One is Sean's age and the other a little younger.

Maggie said, "You might get a call to change diapers because Sloan will be out that night and Russ is out of town. Sloan's father is 85 and he'll be babysitting."

"So, why will I get a call?"

"Because Sloan's father is 85 and he doesn't do that sort of thing."

I asked, "So whose diaper will I be changing?"

His latest syntax error is saying "is it" instead of "isn't it."

"Daddy, snow is cold—is it?"

The children in the night's din are screeching. I can hear them a few family yards away. Screaming bloody murder. They howl in terror and horror. This is how they have fun, of course.

Having kids changes everything. I now rate restaurants by the quality of their crayons.

60 MONTHS

Leap's Phonics Library is an educational toy kind of like an alphabet keyboard. Six functions. You can learn one letter at a time or
whole words or play music. Another option is a three-letter word
button. You spell a three-letter word and then a woman's voice tells
you what word you spelled.
Maggie went out to a parent-teacher seminar to discuss the chal-
lenges facing the school system. The following morning she called
me at work.
"Thanks," she said.
In the background I could hear Sean playing with the keyboard and
laughing. The female phonics voice kept repeating the word "ass."

The Pledge of Allegiance . . . they still make them say this to begin
their school day.
*I pledge allegiance to the flag of the United States of America and
to the republic for which it stands: one nation under God, indivisible,
with liberty and justice for all.*
   "Sean, do you know what indivisible means?"
   "Yeah—it means in the United States you are invisible."
Public education setting the bar high.

Sean: "We got goody bags at school. Here's a cotton ball."
Dad: "What do you use a cotton ball for?"
Sean: "You put it on a stick and pretend you're roasting a marsh-
mallow."

It's weird, but five-year-olds can beat parents when they all go to
the bowling alley.

"Daddy, I'm all clean now—I wiped my hands on my pants."

(the same way he was conceived) 159

Dad: "What was the best thing that happened in school today?"
Sean: "Recess."

Children are taught to sing the alphabet long enough to adequately wash their hands under a faucet. Most versions go like this: "A, B, C, D, E, F, G ... at this point the tempo speeds up quite a bit ..."hblaaeeebbbammm Z!"
Done. Without drying.

My wife re-engineered one of Sean's toys: the shaved ice maker for lemonade. She added vodka. The next morning clutching a cup of coffee, she locked herself in the bedroom and told me she won't be doing that again.

Kids love questions. They also love asking the same question over and over.
"Daddy, why are there holes in a tennis racket?"
"Daddy, why are there holes in a tennis racket?"
"Daddy, why are there holes in a tennis racket?"

Maggie took Sean up the coast to visit her parents for the weekend. Here are a few things I accomplished while they were away.
1. Never use a paint roller with a cat at your feet.
2. I got take-out Bar-B-Q ribs and ate them in the car like a weasel protecting her pups. Seriously—there were splatter marks on the inside of the windshield like a crime scene.
3. I realized the other day, "I get to throw stuff out!"
I'm going around the house with a wheel barrel throwing out all Mommy's old magazines and papers. And then I reconsidered using a paper shredder; that way there can be no evidence. Whenever I throw anything out, no matter how small, Maggie goes dumpster diving. I've seen her stand next to a can holding up a stained sock from a three year old—with cat hair on it.

Our Baby Was Born Premature

"This could go to the Salvation Army!"
I tell her, "How can an organization having the words Salvation and Army in the same name not be suspect?"
Shredding or burning. It's the only way to go.

I did my ritual sneaking-the-beer-into-my-coffee-mug that I take to the park when Sean wants to play. My neighbor, Russ, does the same thing. We watch our kids and check out the nursing moms.

It seems like all we do is go to birthday parties. Children are going to three parties a week now, which is more than KISS in their heyday. And they all have cake and ice cream and candy and pizza.
Some of the parties have themes. We went to a four-year-old's birthday party and all the kids had knight armor including swords. Always good for their eyes.
Pinatas. Another great idea. Let's teach children to smash the hell out of something with a stick or pole until it cracks, and then watch the hysteria as all the kids fight over candy, leaving the smallest kid who didn't get any to ball his eyes out.
The question remains: should I lay down the law or just sit back under the steamroller of corporate sameness and drink alcohol like all the other parents?

AND THEN THERE WAS T-BALL . . .

We had opening Day in the park for Sean's baseball league.
Sean is on the T-ball Yankees in the NRLL: North Redondo Little
League. And it is true, the kids on his team are all little. At our first
coaches meeting in the field with the part-time league commis-
sioner full-time mom present—I secretly tried to locate the *T-ball
Jock Dad*. It wasn't long before I found him.
"So now you're taking away our practice time!" he shrilled as his
belly hung out of his shirt. We listened to various safety instructions
and league rules including a lesson on how to teach the kids to hit
and catch and you could hear a pin drop. It was time for my question to the group.
"During the game—if your first baseman is sitting and drawing circles in the sand with his finger—should we encourage him to draw
better pictures?"
Tough crowd.
I volunteered to be the T-ball Yankee's coach. The kids seem to like
me especially when I chase them around the bases pretending to
eat them.
Our first game is on Saturday and I guess whichever team has less
flu wins.

Practice was salvaged despite only six kids making it out of nine.
1st Practice Highlights:
– We had to tell Luke and Sean, "Don't throw the glove—throw the
ball!"
– Samantha jumped up and down on the spot for most of the prac-
tice (she likes Sean).
– I showed up with 12 balls. Left with 8 balls.
– My left fielder chased a butterfly while the ball bounced by her.
I guess that means it went well.

Our Baby Was Born Premature

I have discovered the indifferent parent, already. One father left the practice. He said, "Its cold out here I'm going home."

IT'S REDONDO BEACH, CALIFORNIA. I've never seen parents like this, shivering in a sunny park. They must have immigrated from a volcano.

One of the mom's is a trap door spider. She waits to pounce on you and then completely stresses you out with questions.

"Oh God—when is this practice over!? I have a nail appointment!"

All the moms on the T-ball Yankees are on medication for depression—that's my guess.

"It's so cold."

"There are so many rules."

"I can't make it to practice because my kid has music lessons."

I haven't seen a girl named Kari since the first practice. Her mother is a single mom. She opened up to me on the phone one night. "I usually don't answer emails—I have hundreds of them in my inbox. My boyfriend is a pitcher but he's not on the scene and I have four kids. I'm a widow."

Our name should be the T-ball Train Wrecks.

I hope she hasn't wasted her $160 T-ball registration. I told her, "I find that beer helps at T-ball practice."

I showed up for our third practice and one kid looked like he had already been crying for about an hour. He had no baseball glove either. I asked his mom, "Where's his glove?"

She's wearing sunglasses.

"Oh, sorry, I forgot it at home."

That kid lasted about five minutes before he bit another kid and then went home. And where's the dad? What kind of father sends his child to a baseball practice with no glove? I'll tell you; a father who's a child.

(the same way he was conceived) 163

I awoke early on the morning of our first T-ball game and went to the park to help set up. I wanted to watch the first game between two other teams in order get a feeling of what to expect and how to handle it. Luckily for them I showed up. Only one other dad was there. I helped him rake the field.

Our game was at 11:30 a.m. and everybody showed up except for the kid with the single mom that has four kids. The Dad's who volunteered to be assistant coaches arrived and commandeered the players. I told jokes to the parents behind the fence in the bleachers.

"Just to let everybody know—you will need to submit a form for your kid to test for steroid use. And don't worry; the chalk lines on the field are nontoxic and edible."

By the beginning of the third inning most of my fielders were turning in circles on the spot because they were hungry and had to pee. The game ended and as I was walking from the out-field my assistant coach said, "Okay—now we'll line up the kids on the base line and say our appreciation cheer before giving the other team high fives and then we're done."

At that moment he looked over my shoulder and said, "Oh well?"

Maggie had already distributed the after game snacks to our players and pretzels were flying everywhere in a frenzy of squealing.

At our first practice after our first game a father showed up with his son, Dylan. He must have come straight from work because the guy was wearing a button-up shirt shiny dress shoes and seemed like he was in a hurry to go somewhere else. He wanted Dylan to throw him the ball and held out his new baseball glove.

"C'mon Dylan throw the ball!"

Dylan looked his father dead in the eye, and on purpose, dropped the ball at his own feet.

His father closed his eyes and began to tremble. I took over with Dylan as his father left the field of play.

Game 2 was a tremendous success. Everyone showed up and the kids ran much better than the first game. Some highlights:

– Sean B. trapped a blistering hit and was able to throw the ball to first base, which was successfully manned by Kishav for our first out of the season.

– While standing in right field, Sean A. (my son) made sure to tell the coach that he had found candy in his back pocket.

– I asked Savanah, while she was playing short stop, what she was drawing in the dirt with her finger, and she looked up at me: "Two."

– The Diamondbacks had to call a timeout because Luchio was running in from center field to show his mom something; one of his teeth fell out.

I asked Sean what he liked best about the baseball game and he said, "When I went home and found the skateboard Mommy bought me."

The kids were just beginning to get the baseball thing (like where the positions are) and then the league decided to give the teams a Spring Break for 5 weeks.

Our first game in the second season finally came—and it meant we had to do field set up. I got up at 6 a.m. and did my batting order at the kitchen table. I had a feeling all the parents and coaches were going to totally flake in apathy and that the field would be a mess since it hadn't been prepped in over a month. I showed early and with my trusty locker key I got into the field tools and cart to drag the field, place the bases, and use the chalk caddy. It took me an hour with the 9 a.m game start-time creeping up. Another dad showed up when I was putting the finishing touches on the pitcher's mound. It felt good. I was right about the adult apathy but I successfully set up a baseball field by myself, including a pretty good pitchers mound circle. All there was left to do was water the field down, which the only other dad there took on sheepishly. Fifteen minutes to game time; the parents all started straggling on to the field with fear in their eyes and Starbucks in their hands.

(the same way he was conceived) 165

Our first game back was against the Padres. Most kids had for-gotten how to catch and where to throw. With two kids short, we ventured on and played the other team. It was pretty even except for that thing where all the fielders try to get the bouncing ball after its hit and wrestle each other for it. In the third and last inning of play, little Makayla was my pitcher and Keshav was on first base (our two best players). To my astonishment, Makayla caught the grounder from the Padre's batter and she threw it straight to first base and Keshav, with his foot on the base, stretched for the ball and caught it. A great out; **my** goal of getting one or two outs at first base during the season was met. I could quit now.

The last game of the season was against the Red Sox and the Evil Coach from Hell—actually a husband-wife team. Way too Alpha. The kind of coaches that use words like "Drills," "Execute," and "Win-ners will be crowned!" The guy wears *Terminator* wrap-around sun-glasses and he teaches his kids to "tag" everybody out. I was losing sleep over it and sent out this email prior to game day...

Hello All,
It always helps to have a team parent help out on first base (to point our player in the direction of second base,) and in the dugout when we bat. I have tried to rotate players to keep their interest for our last three-inning game of the season.
Thanks to Brian T., Jose S., Sam B., and Dan for all your help this season.
The Red Sox coach likes to have his kids "tag" everybody, which tends to confuse the players and me. However, I think our players are ready ... not sure if I am though.
p.

Well, all the parents showed and the opposing coaches, the hus-band and wife duo, looked eager get the game underway. It started out bad. Keshav, my star player, took a line drive in the belly and went down in tears but he got up shortly and shook it off.

I could sense the coach and his wife from the Red Sox snickering in glee. Then my son, Sean, tried unsuccessfully as pitcher to tag out the base runner to first, instead of throwing it to first. He yelled at everyone on the field, "My daddy said it's okay to tag the player out!"

And, head hung low, I hid not-so-well under my sunglasses and slouched back to the dugout.

Maggie was on the bench.

"He busted you."

The Red Sox were winning and I was starting to get an overwhelming feeling of battle fatigue. The second inning went a little smoother. During my last batter—who gets an automatic home run per league rules—the Red Sox coach had all his kids waltz off the field while she was still rounding the bases.

" I hate this dickhead," I said to myself.

The third inning came—along with my prayers. To my joy all my kids hit off the pitch and beat it out to first base. We went up by a run. I pitched two "imaginary balls" to my son, which he pretended to hit over the fence. A little game we often practice. The Red Sox coach was stunned. Our defense was even better. We had two successful outs at first base, and then their ace hitter came up to bat. It happened so fast I still can't believe it—an out-of-the-blue moment and a play I won't forget for quite awhile. The kid cracked a pop fly ball. Keshav—my player who got hurt in the first inning and was now my pitcher—caught the fly ball for the greatest out of the year. The bleachers filled with six T-Ball Yankee parents erupted in cheers. I looked over my shoulder out at second base. The Red Sox coach had his Terminator sunglasses off and was arguing with his kid—who was crying.

Victory was ours.

(the same way he was conceived)   167

We decided to move to our house in Canada. Sean will probably want to play hockey, and just before he steps onto the ice for the first time, wearing hundreds of dollars of equipment, I will grab his shoulder pad and say, "There are only 900 guys in the NHL—are you sure you don't want to be an entomologist?"

Only in Canada do people get up at 5 a.m. when its 10 below zero in Feb and say, "Let's go to a refrigerated building!" And like in any minor league, hopefully the kids will rise above the example set by their parents. How about having more referees in the stands than on the ice. Perhaps I'll find an over-80 hockey league? I need an advantage.

My friend Jeff, a single father who has an 11-year-old boy and a teenage daughter warned me how fast kids grow and to enjoy it while you have it. He said, "The week is slow but the year is fast."

Acknowledgments

I'd like to thank Sean and Maggie O'Neill for all the material I stole from them. I would also like to thank my managing editor, Gary Anderson, for believing in my worms. Thank God he has spell check.

About the Author

Paul Alexander is a comedian who has appeared on MTV, A&E, and Comedy Central. He worked in Film Production for a couple of decades. Paul never had an affair on his wife or abandoned his kids for the sake of his career in Hollywood, which is why he now works as a baker in the middle of a Canadian island.

9 781732 709768